Instructional Models

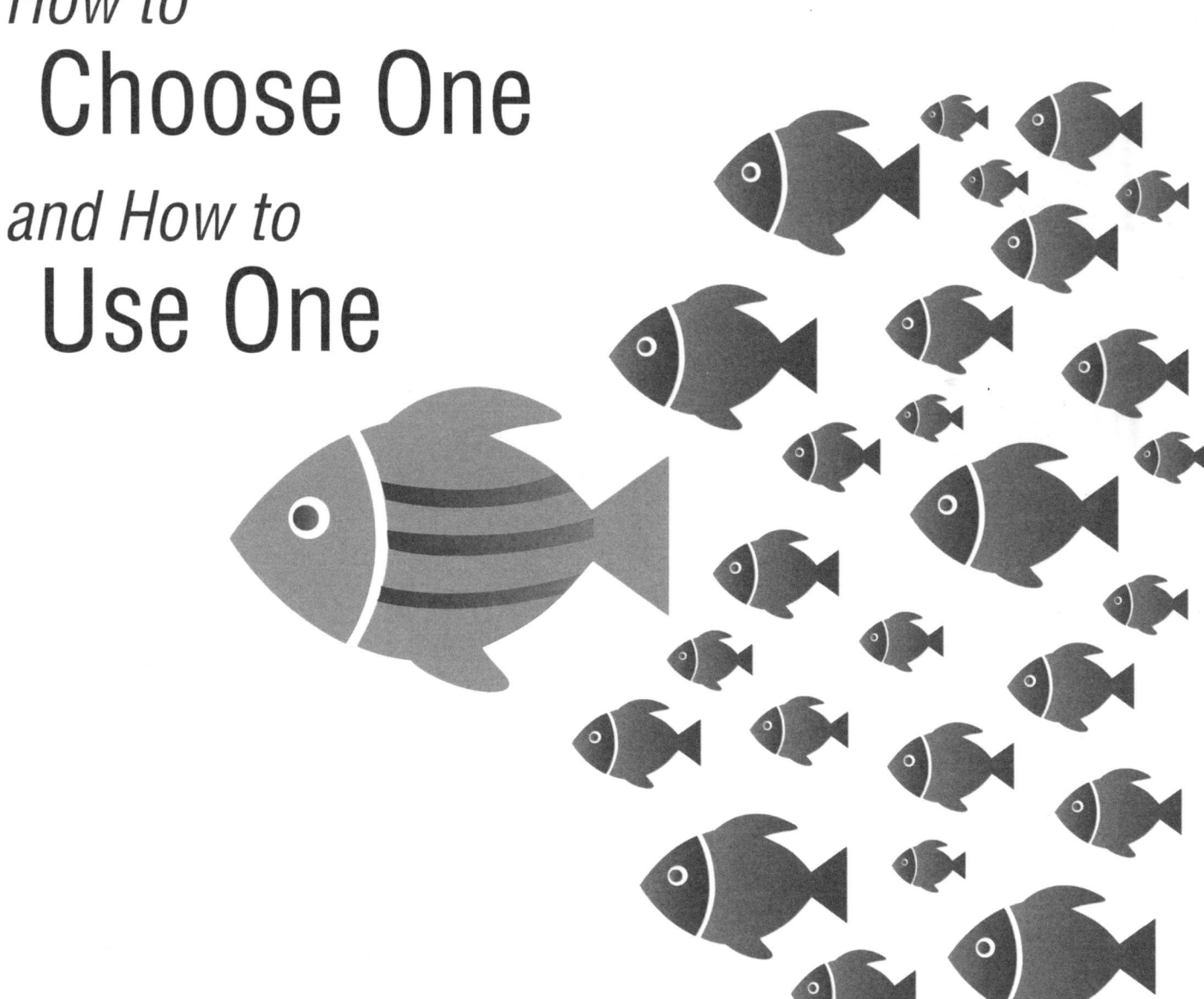

How to **Choose One**
and How to **Use One**

McREL INTERNATIONAL
Denver, Colorado USA

Elizabeth Ross HUBBELL | Bryan GOODWIN

McREL INTERNATIONAL

McREL International

4601 DTC Boulevard, Suite 500

Denver, CO 80237 USA

Phone: 303.337.0990 | Fax: 303.337.3005

Website: www.mcrel.org | Email: info@mcrel.org | Store: store.mcrel.org

Copyright © 2019 by McREL International. All rights reserved. No part of this publication may be reproduced or transmitted in any form or by any means without the prior written permission of the publisher.

About McREL

McREL International helps educators flourish by turning research into solutions that transform teaching, learning, and leading. As a nonprofit, nonpartisan education research and development organization, McREL provides practical, effective guidance and training for teachers and education leaders across the U.S. and around the world.

All referenced trademarks are the property of the respective owners. All internet links mentioned in this book are correct as of the initial publication date.

Printed in the United States of America.

To order, visit store.mcrel.org

ISBN: 978-1-7326994-4-1

Library of Congress Control Number: 2019906817

Hubbell, E. R., & Goodwin, B. (2019). *Instructional models: How to choose one and how to use one*. Denver, CO: McREL International.

Instructional Models
How to Choose One *and How to* Use One

List of Tools iv

Introduction: Getting it right from the beginning 1

Chapter 1: The power of instructional design models 4

Chapter 2: Knowing better and *doing* better 13

Chapter 3: Choosing the right model for you 18

Chapter 4: Planning for successful professional learning 35

Chapter 5: Managing and overcoming resistance to change 57

Chapter 6: Measuring progress toward success 73

Chapter 7: Building on your foundation 92

Chapter 8: Doing the right things right 101

Appendix: If you're on your own 107

References 111

About the Authors 115

List of Tools

Tools to evaluate instructional models

Tool 1: Using instructional rounds to find bright spots 31

Tool 2: Connecting observational data and student data 32

Tool 3: Sample rubric for evaluating instructional models 34

Tool 4: Deciding on your approach to professional learning 50

Tool 5: Professional learning planning worksheet 52

Tool 6: Creating an innovation configuration map 54

Tool 7: Inviting feedback protocol 55

Tool 8: Peer coaching conversation protocol 56

Tools to assist in managing and overcoming resistance to change

Tool 9: Responding to concerns or resistance 70

Tool 10: Planning to overcome resistance to change 72

Tools for measuring and monitoring progress

Tool 11: Creating a logic model 90

Tools for building on your foundation

Tool 12: Cross-referencing current models with new initiatives 99

Tool 13: Dialogue exercise—Why are we doing what we're doing? 100

Introduction: Getting it right from the beginning

The idea for this book was born out of our many years of serving as consultants and seeing the promise and peril of instructional models—the powerful gains schools can experience when they use instructional models to support greater consistency in teaching quality as well as the myriad ways in which these efforts can come off the rails.

The schools and districts that had the most success started with a needs assessment to determine what model would best suit their needs. They were careful to get input from all levels of faculty and staff. Most importantly, they were strategic in their timing and training to ensure the change effort had the best chance of success. Finally, they implemented both formative and summative evaluation methods to track the success and impact of their framework.

While these steps seem simple and intuitive, it's easy to dismiss their importance when there is so much work to be done and so little time in the school year to do it. We watch students and teachers struggle and we want to do something *right away* to be helpful.

How we've designed this book

This book should be a companion as you implement a schoolwide instructional model. The first two chapters establish why instructional models are so important—and why organizational challenges can put them out of reach. True to our belief in the power of checklists as do-confirm lists (reminding us of what's most important) (Goodwin & Hubbell, 2013), each subsequent chapter will include a series of steps or actions that we recommend for success and tools to help you accomplish them.

◊ Step 1: Choosing the right model for you

We first recommend that you take a broad survey of the instructional models that are available. In chapter 3, we provide a brief overview of several current and classic instructional models and suggestions for the problems they are designed to solve. This book is designed to be model-agnostic—to be used with whichever model you deem most fitting to your current needs. The chapter also provides suggestions for how to make this choice. One mistake school leaders often make is not getting enough input and perspectives on the choice of model. We see this happening often: A school leader learns of a new model, gets excited about it, and tries to force the model on his or her faculty.

What we have found to be much more successful is when a designated team of educators first conducts a needs assessment in order to identify their key issues in instruction, then does a thorough audit of the research and tools that are available to help them solve their problem. This chapter will provide suggested procedures and tools for doing so.

◊ Step 2: Planning for successful professional learning

Another common error is cramming the professional learning into one or two intense sessions. Changing practice and seeing the impact your instructional modifications have on student learning takes time and focus. We have found the most successful implementations have started with a broad overview followed by small, "bite-sized" professional learning sessions, each with time to implement, experiment, and reflect on what was learned. These are ideally run through professional learning communities that are built around collegial discussions and reflection. So chapter 4 provides a suggested timeline for implementing an instructional model. In this chapter, we will go through the roles and responsibilities of leaders during an implementation, from principal to staff development coordinators to teacher leaders. For any initiative to be successful, your instructional leaders need to be as knowledgeable, if not more so, on the chosen model as your faculty. This chapter will outline suggestions for training your instructional leaders and their various roles as the model is implemented. There is also a section that describes how to implement at a larger level, such as district or systemwide.

◊ Step 3: Managing and overcoming resistance to change

No matter how good the model, how much input you solicit from faculty, or how open-minded your educators, there will always be stumbling blocks as you implement change. In chapter 5, we help you identify the reason for the challenge, whether it is from fear of change, lack of knowledge, or a philosophical disagreement. Your initiative's success will depend on having a critical mass of your faculty on board. This chapter provides steps to help you get there.

◊ Step 4: Measuring progress toward success

Drawing from Covey's (1989) philosophy of beginning with the end in mind, in chapter 6 we provide suggestions for identifying your criteria for success. We recommend this be a collaborative effort with faculty, instructional leaders, and school leaders. By agreeing as a group on success criteria, leadership teams can set the expectation from the very beginning that the effort reflects a professional learning community holding one another accountable while supporting each other along the way.

◊ Step 5: Building on your foundation

No matter how impactful your instructional model is, there will come a point when either the initiative no longer needs such intense focus because it has become a part of the organizational norms, or you're ready to *adapt* the model you've adopted, making shared changes to your approach. Or new challenges may emerge that prompt you to recalibrate your priorities in order to address them. Chapter 7 will help you make such decisions with integrity and transparency.

◊ **Extra material: If you're on your own**

Most of this book assumes that a school leader (or leadership team) is guiding the effort with the positional authority and influence to make change happen. Sometimes, though, an individual faculty member, teacher leader, or small group of teachers may become convinced that a consistent instructional design model is a solution to a school's challenges, yet struggle to get others interested in learning more about the model. The appendix will help those who are operating on their own and must influence without positional authority.

Enjoy the journey!

We are excited that you have chosen to take this journey with us to better meet the needs of your students and teachers. Following these steps, we feel confident that you can make an impact on student learning while also creating a dynamic professional learning organization. Let's dive in!

Chapter 1: The power of instructional design models

For as long as most educators can remember, schools nearly everywhere have engaged in the annual ritual of drafting hefty school improvement plans. These often include literally dozens of things school leaders commit their teams to doing in an effort to improve student outcomes—or at least to persuade the powers that be that they are busily going about the business of improvement.

There's just one problem.

Too often, those improvement plans don't translate into noticeable improvement that can be sustained over time, despite the best intentions and efforts by teachers and principals. Nationwide, after initial gains under the high-stakes testing regime of No Child Left Behind, scores on the National Assessment of Educational Program (NAEP) have plateaued.

So then, too many politicians and news stories would have us believe, our nation's schools must be predominantly bad, right?

Not so fast.

Our experience over decades of visiting and working with hundreds of schools far and wide tells us that it's actually pretty hard to find a thoroughly bad school. Most teachers in most schools do, in fact, know how to teach. Most principals do, in fact, know how to keep a campus running. Most schools are, in fact, really trying hard to do the right things for their students.

But if they're mostly doing the right things, then why aren't more schools able to make significant gains in achievement, and hold on to them?

Maybe it's because those small errors, the not quite doing the right things right, add up over the course of a school year.

We believe this to be the case.

Ours is not a merely philosophical stance nor wishful thinking, but rather, an empirical judgment born out of working with and analyzing schools nationwide that have significantly improved student learning. Not by forcing students to drop out, firing hordes of teachers, adopting high-tech gadgetry, or getting students to sit in straight rows and chant along with the teachers, but rather, by simply getting everyone in the school focused on doing one thing that matters most. As it turns out, that *one thing*—that single, critical leverage point for improving schools—can be easy to overlook, often because it remains hidden in plain sight. Uncover it, and your school or district will start doing the right things right.

Quality instruction in every classroom

Years ago, researchers in Louisiana (Reynolds, Stringfield, & Schaffer, 2001) sent observers out to a collection of schools that were alike in nearly every respect, serving similar students in similar communities with similar levels of funding. There was just one difference. In one set of schools, students were performing at much *higher* levels than expected; in the other set of schools, students were performing at much *lower* levels. In hopes of discovering what distinguished the two groups, the researchers asked the observers (mostly non-educator laypeople) to tour the schools, record their observations, and report back what they saw.

To avoid biasing the observers, the researchers kept it a secret which schools were higher- and which were lower-performing. Interestingly, nearly all of the observers could identify the better-performing schools. Bear in mind, they had no obvious clues to tip them off. The higher-performing schools weren't any wealthier, nor did they serve more privileged students than the lower-performing ones. Nor were they bedecked with high-tech gadgets or engaged in the latest reform du jour. In fact, as the researchers put it, they were as "plain vanilla" as could be.

So, what were they doing differently?

Simply this: *They were focused on delivering consistent, high-quality instruction.* In the high-performing schools, observers saw teachers providing challenging, engaging instruction and students focused on learning *in every classroom*. Meanwhile, in the low-performing schools, there were some great teachers sprinkled here and there, to be sure. Yet often, in the very next classroom, they'd see uninspiring instruction and off-task student behaviors. In short, to paraphrase Forrest Gump, classrooms in low-performing schools were like a box of chocolates: "You never know what you're gonna get."

International researchers discovered something similar when comparing the differences between high-performing school systems and mediocre ones. As it turns out, the most salient feature of high-performing school systems was the presence of *consistent* instructional quality. As the researchers wrote, "Top-performing systems recognize that the only way to improve outcomes is to improve instruction; learning occurs when teachers and students interact, and thus to improve learning implies improving the quality of that interaction" (Barber & Mourshed, 2007, p. 26).

Sadly, such consistency is far from reality in U.S. schools. While examining the educational experiences of nearly 1,000 elementary students from across the U.S., a team at the University of Virginia (Pianta, Belsky, Houts, & Morrison, 2007) found wide variance in the quality of instruction these students were receiving. In fact, only *7% of students* received high-quality instruction and emotional support in all three grade levels they studied (first, third, and fifth). Moreover, in disproportionate numbers, low-income students were far more likely than higher-income students to experience weak instruction and emotional support in their classrooms.

Ending chutes and ladders

What all of this suggests is that an important key—indeed, perhaps *the most important key*—to improving school performance is guaranteeing that every classroom in the school provides high-quality learning experiences for students so that their success isn't left to chance or the luck of the draw based upon their placement in teachers' classrooms. For too many students, though, schools often reflect something of a cruel game of chutes and ladders; one year they get a good teacher and climb to new heights of learning, then the very next year, they receive ineffective instruction and slide right back down again. Sadly, as William Sanders (Sanders & Rivers, 1996) discovered years ago when analyzing student performance across multiple grade levels, receiving an ineffective teacher three years in a row—riding a three-year chute downwards—can result in a loss of learning from which students never recover.

So, if this seems obvious enough—that consistent, high-quality teaching is the key to a good school—why is it so hard to make it happen?

Missing the mark

For starters, a perennial problem in education is that, as numerous studies have found, professional learning (PL) for teachers—sending teachers to hours of workshops, seminars, or giving them online tools and teacher videos in the name of improving their professional practice—typically does little to change teachers' practice.

Another common fix—teacher evaluation systems—has generated similarly disappointing results. Over the past decade or more, districts nearly everywhere have developed or adopted newfangled systems to evaluate teacher performance based on complex calculations of student growth and teachers' ability to incorporate multiple, often dozens, of elements of effective teaching into their classrooms. It all seems sensible enough—turn up the heat on teachers and they'll teach better. Right?

Perhaps not. Few studies to date have shown that the enormous time and energy devoted to implementing these systems have done much to improve teaching practice or raise student achievement (Darling-Hammond, Amrein-Beardsley, Haertel, & Rothstein, 2012). At issue may be the fact that teacher evaluation instruments are often, in the words of school improvement consultant and author Mike Schmoker (2014), so "complex," "bloated," and "jargon-laced" that they fail to provide teachers with much clarity about how to design and deliver better learning experiences for students. In short, while these complex systems may give teachers and principals plenty to worry about and discuss, they're often so broad and complicated that they fail to provide specific guidance or clarity about what good instruction looks like in the classroom. More to the point, rarely do these systems describe how teachers ought to sequence learning to help students acquire new knowledge and skills, providing them with, in a word, a *model* for teaching and learning.

The difference between frameworks and models

At this point, you may be thinking, *No, we have that. We have the [fill in the blank] teacher evaluation system.* Here, we want to be clear: Most teacher evaluation systems *aren't actually instructional models*, but, at best, frameworks of teaching practice. We know it may sound like we're splitting hairs, so bear with us as we spend a moment to parse the difference between two terms that get used interchangeably, yet have decidedly different meanings.

Frameworks arrange and structure declarative (factual) knowledge into categories, taxonomies, or mental "buckets." In literature, for example, we use a mental framework to distinguish among various genres of fiction (mystery, action, romance, and so forth). In biology, we use a taxonomy first developed by Aristotle to categorize different types of living organisms (plants, mammals, reptiles, fish, and so on). With this in mind, we can see that most teacher evaluation systems are *frameworks* that categorize the myriad things we want teachers to attend to in their classrooms and professional lives; they clarify *what* to do, yet not necessarily *how* to do it.

Models, on the other hand, explain how things work, often by describing a process, cycle, or sequence of events. For example, meteorologists understand the water cycle as a shared mental model that describes how water evaporates from the ocean, condenses into clouds, and returns to the earth as precipitation. Similarly, astronomers use a model of the solar system to understand and describe how planets rotate on their axes and revolve around the sun and how moons revolve around planets and so on. In film and theater, playwrights and screenwriters often follow the model of a three-act play to sequence a series of scenes into narratives with rising action, conflict, resolution, and denouement. Mental models help us understand abstract processes. They can also be used to replicate works based on a theory.

In fact, for many intellectual endeavors, models provide us with examples to follow or emulate. To further illustrate this difference, McREL has actually created both a *framework for instruction* and a *model for learning*. In *Classroom Instruction That Works* (Dean, Hubbell, Pitler, & Stone, 2012) we grouped 23 high-yield instructional strategies into nine categories of effective instruction and ultimately the following three-component **framework**:

1. Creating the environment for learning
2. Helping students develop understanding, and
3. Helping students extend and apply knowledge.

This framework, however, doesn't *describe* the process of learning or how the strategies could be sequenced to support the process of learning; rather, it's designed to help educators go from having a disorganized "grab bag" of teaching tips and tricks to a more organized and robust toolkit of research-based strategies to apply in their classrooms.

We know from working with thousands of educators worldwide that this framework has been immensely helpful to arrange and sharpen their thinking about pedagogy. However, it doesn't describe *how* to sequence teaching strategies into lessons or unit design (or *why* these strategies work or *when* to use them).

In a recent white paper and forthcoming book, *Student Learning That Works*, we provide educators with a six-phase **model** for lesson and unit design based on the science of learning—in particular, what cognitive scientists call the *information processing model*. As a model, it shows the sequence of mental activities—from start to finish—required for students to turn new information into long-term memory. See the table on p. 8 for an alignment of *Classroom Instruction That Works* to a learning model.

Table 1. Aligning *Classroom Instruction That Works* to a learning model

Student Learning That Works phases of learning	*Classroom Instruction That Works* strategies	*Classroom Instruction That Works* categories
Become interested	Cues Advance organizers Questions	Cues, questions, and advanced organizers
Commit to learning	Setting objectives Reinforcing effort Providing recognition	Setting objectives and providing feedback Reinforcing effort and providing recognition
Focus on new knowledge	Pictures and pictographs Mental images Note taking Graphic organizers Models and manipulatives Kinesthetic movement	Nonlinguistic representations Summarizing and note taking
Make sense of learning	Comparing Questions Classifying Cooperative learning Summarizing	Identifying similarities and differences Cooperative learning Summarizing and note taking
Practice and rehearse	Assigning homework Providing practice Providing feedback	Assigning homework and providing practice Setting objectives and providing feedback
Extend and apply	Problem solving Experimental inquiry Systems analysis Investigation	Generating and testing hypotheses

Essentially, models help us to make sense of procedural (*how-to*) knowledge by explaining how things work or *how to* do something. In fact, for many intellectual endeavors, models provide us with examples to follow or imitate.

So, why does that matter? Well, because as we'll see, one of the most effective ways to develop talent—in any area—is to follow a model based on science or accumulated experience (expertise).

How people get better: Imitating models

Years ago, a team led by Benjamin Bloom (1956), an icon in education research, studied 120 immensely talented people—pianists, sculptors, tennis players, Olympic swimmers, mathematicians, and neurologists—to figure out what they did that others did not—how they developed their talents while others stagnated. Bloom and his team found that talented people followed remarkably similar progressions or phases of development, including a critical transition from a period of informal training (either learning on their own or with easygoing coaches who nurtured their interests) to a period of "digging in" (p. 437) under the tutelage of more exacting teachers or coaches who helped them master the skills of their discipline, bit by bit, often through a process of imitation.

During this phase, musicians, for example, learned to play others' songs with precision—with the same rhythm and intonation. Artists developed their skills by trying to replicate, often down to exacting detail, the work of the masters. Athletes dissected and copied the techniques of the pros. Similarly, as a young man, Benjamin Franklin developed his acumen as a writer by reconstructing articles he admired, word for word, from memory, comparing his draft with the original to unearth his own faults (Ericsson, Prietula, & Cokely, 2007). Through this process, he improved his writing abilities and eventually became an accomplished writer under the nom de plume Poor Richard.

What imitation does more than anything else is shorten our learning curve: Instead of spending countless hours casting about to figure out how to do something well, we simply learn from others' expertise—which likely took them countless hours to figure out how to do.

Teachers are no different. One of the most powerful ways to help them learn how to deliver consistent, high-quality instruction is to provide them with an instructional design model—a common understanding of how to design and deliver "mastery learning" opportunities for students. *Mastery learning* is another term that gets bandied about and used in different ways, but generally speaking it reflects a sequence of learning activities that includes at least some of these elements:

- setting clear learning objectives,
- using an "anticipatory set" to focus and engage students in learning,
- presenting or modeling new knowledge and/or skills,
- providing students with opportunities to practice new knowledge or skills,
- checking for student understanding,
- reteaching as needed to address targeted learning needs, and
- confirming understanding before moving to new content (Guskey, 2007; Hunter, 1985).

Over the last few decades, researchers have found that consistent application of instructional models that reflect mastery learning has powerful effects on student learning. A meta-analysis of 108 studies, for example, found that students in mastery learning settings achieved 20 percentile points higher on subsequent tests of knowledge than students in non-mastery settings (Kulik, Kulik, Bangert-Drowns, & Slavin, 1990). Hattie (2011) similarly found one of the most powerful effect sizes among 800 meta-analyses of research on education to be the use of the Direct Instruction program developed by Dr. Siegfried Engelmann, Dr. Wesley Becker, and colleagues. Direct Instruction employs a sequence of learning similar to the mastery learning model.

Models provide a shared "operating system"

Common models of instruction appear to support greater consistency and better quality of instruction in schools and districts by creating a common "operating system" for teaching and learning, not unlike how a common operating system on computers and smartphones (e.g., Apple iOS, Microsoft Windows, Android) supports a wide variety of applications and inter-communication. Helping teachers to develop a shared vocabulary and understanding of instructional design supports the creation of a common platform for sharing lesson plans and engaging in professional collaboration; that is, when every teacher in a school approaches lesson and unit planning in similar ways, it's much easier to share lessons with one another.

As it turns out, that's exactly what many turnaround schools do. In a series of case studies, Chenoweth (2007, 2009) found that a key way many turnaround schools dramatically improved student performance was by compiling and sharing exemplary lesson plans, something that's, of course, more feasible if teachers use a common model for lesson design. In these schools, novice teachers aren't left to their own devices in a mad scramble to develop 180 days of new lessons (likely of uneven quality) for their students, but instead can draw upon the collective wisdom of more expert teachers in the building. A study of nearly 400 teachers, in fact, found that giving teachers access to better lessons as well as an online support group for implementing them had an effect size equivalent to moving students from classrooms with average (50th percentile) teachers to accomplished (80th percentile) ones—with an even larger (*double*) effect size for bottom quartile teachers (Jackson & Makarin, 2018).

Yet despite the obvious benefit of giving teachers great lessons to follow (and learn how to design their own solid lessons in the process of following the models), many schools and districts fail to provide teachers with these resources; a survey of Teach for America teachers in 31 states, for example, found that only 15% reported having access to high-quality instructional materials, like lesson plans (Mathews, 2011).

Models help us collaborate as professionals

Here, we should add that instructional design models aren't about "dumbing down," "teacher proofing" classrooms, or giving teachers mindless checklists to follow. Far from it. An instructional design model should serve to develop a deep, shared understanding among professionals about how learning works and how a broad repertoire of teaching strategies can support it. It's not meant to be rigid or to limit teachers' creativity, but rather, to serve as a guide for teachers' professional choices, encouraging them to reflect on, and consider at each step along the way, which teaching strategy is most appropriate for what they are trying to help students do in any given phase of a lesson or unit. Similar to a seasoned chef who may well know how to make béarnaise sauce but improvises to better fit a particular vegetable or time of year, we encourage any "recipe" for teaching to allow for—even to expect—professionals to have the freedom to adjust or pivot as needed.

In this regard, an instructional design model should help teachers develop their own mental models for learning and instruction, which is the hallmark of expertise and professionalism—knowing not only what works, but why it works. In turn, teaching professionals can use their mental models to diagnose and solve problems. If, for example, teachers find students are struggling to grasp a particular concept, instead of teaching the same lesson all over again (doing the same thing and expecting different results), they could contemplate which part of the learning might have been inadequate or even overlooked. Perhaps students simply needed more time to make sense of a new idea or more opportunities to participate in guided practice of a new skill.

Teacher preparation programs often fail to develop an understanding of instructional design

At this point, you may be thinking, *Well, our teachers learned how to design effective lessons in their teacher prep programs, right?* Well, maybe not. According to an analysis of 500-plus teacher education programs across the U.S., *just 15%* of these programs ensured their candidates can meet the challenges of designing effective instruction for students. Another 27% received a middling grade of helping prospective teachers address "some" of these challenges. That left fully 58% of colleges in the sample leaving teacher candidates unprepared for these challenges (National Council on Teacher Quality, 2014). At issue, according to the report, is that the guidance many teacher colleges give aspiring teachers when it comes to lesson and unit planning is often "unrealistically expansive, overly specific or vague"—or their "terminology is inconsistent," likely because they're not providing teachers with a single model for lesson design, but a hodgepodge of many.

Moreover, if teacher candidates *are* learning about instructional design, they're likely not encountering the science of learning that should undergird effective instructional design. For example, a recent analysis of 48 textbooks used in 219 teacher preparation courses purporting to teach aspiring educators how to design lessons, found that *not a single textbook* covered all six core principles of learning identified by the Institute of Education Sciences: "pairing graphics with words," "linking abstract concepts with concrete representations," "repeatedly alternating problems with their solutions provided and problems that students must solve," "posing probing questions," "distributing practice," and "assessing to boost retention" (Pomerance, Greenberg, & Walsh, 2016, p. vi). These are the strategies that, according to the researchers, ought to serve as the "cognitive bedrock of effective instructional design" (p. 27). Thus, neglecting to teach about instructional design is "no less remiss than a botany textbook that fails to address photosynthesis or an American government text devoid of a discussion of the three branches of government" (p. 5).

The bottom line here is that while some of your teachers may have a solid grasp of instructional design and regularly incorporate this expertise into how they design and provide learning opportunities for students, it's likely that many others do not. Left to their own devices and without an instructional design model to follow, teachers are apt to deliver inconsistent and likely inadequate learning opportunities for students.

What models are *not*: A caveat as you begin your journey

In a provocatively titled essay, "What's Wrong with Madeline Hunter?" Madeline Hunter (1985), creator of the eponymously named "Hunter model" of instruction, identified several "misunderstandings that lead to abuse" of her own instructional model in schools. At the top of her list were leaders who, often with only a superficial understanding of the model, turned it into a cudgel with which to bludgeon teachers into submission, insisting they follow every aspect of the model to a T. What was more important for leaders to do, Hunter insisted, was to engage teachers in conversation about why they chose a particular strategy or elected to design a lesson in a particular way. At the same time, teachers themselves, Hunter noted, often succumbed to the fallacy that "if a little is good, more is better" as they sought to apply elements of the model to the *nth* degree (for example, piling on additional homework in the interest of giving students gobs of independent practice) that pushed particular elements of the lesson well beyond the point of diminishing returns.

Perhaps most important, Hunter noted that, like most models, her own model was deceptively simple in theory, yet vexingly challenging to implement in practice; we might say it's easy to learn, difficult to master. Often, in Hunter's estimation, leaders falsely believed teachers could learn the model in a workshop and then "magically" apply it in their classrooms. In reality, though, teachers need time to learn the model deeply (understanding both what to do and *why* to do it), significant time to practice it, and opportunities to receive feedback from coaches to help refine their practices. Nothing short of that works.

Finally, Hunter added, an instructional model is not an end in itself, but rather, a means to an end—a way to help teachers develop their own expertise by applying research-based practices with consistency in their classrooms. Like Hunter, we view identifying, adopting, and ensuring the consistent use of an instructional model as a *foundational* element, not the pinnacle, of school improvement and teacher talent development. We see instructional models as something akin to the basic song structure (e.g., verse-chorus-verse-chorus-bridge-verse-chorus) or tried-and-true chord progressions (e.g., C-Am-Dm-G) that help songwriters channel their creative energies. And like any great songwriter, as teachers develop their expertise and artistry, they are apt to enhance, or even deviate from, the original model (breaking the "rules" after they've learned them).

Hunter, of course, developed her model—and issued these warnings—decades ago. In the years since, countless schools have, no doubt, attempted to adopt instructional models . . . and many have failed at it. That doesn't make instructional models a bad idea. To the contrary, in our experience working with schools and school districts—including one that recently demonstrated four years (and counting) of the highest student growth rate in the state of Tennessee—we've seen the power of instructional design models, when applied thoughtfully and consistently, to raise school performance and enhance student learning.

This guidebook draws upon the many lessons we've learned over the years while working to support school teams across the nation in applying instructional models in their schools. Like Hunter, we don't view instructional models as silver bullets. In our other writings—see, for example, *Simply Better* (Goodwin, 2011)—we've highlighted better instruction as but one element of doing what matters most. Adopting an instructional design model is a critical element for ensuring more consistent, high-quality instruction and thus, often a good place to begin when improving school performance. Indeed, for many schools, putting an instructional model in place is often *the single most important* step they can take to dramatically improve student achievement—one that, when done right, can not only enhance student learning and engagement, but also create a collegial culture of professionalism.

In the pages that follow, we'll provide practical advice, tools, and questions to ask with colleagues to avoid common pitfalls—and find real success—when using instructional design models to support more consistent instruction, deeper student learning, and professional collaboration in your school.

Chapter 2: Knowing better and *doing* better

If we *know* better, why don't we *do* better? That's a common lament for many attempting to implement better practices in schools. At times, school leaders may blame teachers: Why won't they get on board? Don't they see how important this is? Are they trying to make my life miserable?

The reality though, is that changing professional practices is no small undertaking. Consider what's required when someone asks us to adopt a new professional practice or to follow a new set of complex procedures. We must embrace the new practice, learn about it, and practice it repeatedly until we master it and embed it into our day-to-day routines. On top of that, we often must *unlearn* old behaviors. In short, we must change our *habits*, and as we all know, old habits die hard—whether it's laying off salt, cutting carbs, or weaning ourselves from our smartphones.

So, when we're asking teachers to implement a new instructional model, we are, in effect, asking many people to change many habits at once. To complicate matters, leaders often bring faulty mindsets when it comes to encouraging people to change these habits, which in turn leads them to employ counterproductive leadership behaviors—as we'll illustrate with the following (only partly) fictional tale of two schools whose leaders adopted distinctly different mindsets and leadership strategies for encouraging schoolwide adoption of a learning model.

Tale of two schools

SMOOTH SAILING

In a small, suburban elementary school office, Julia, the principal, sits back and looks out her window. It's a beautiful spring day—not yet too hot, but warm enough to be a reminder of how quickly the school year is coming to a close. She reflects on how well this year has gone. Granted, there were hiccups here and there, but the initiatives she launched in August are well underway and she has seen a huge improvement in instruction since the holiday break.

Just over a year ago, she and her instructional coaches noticed how inconsistently teachers were using key, research-based teaching strategies. Even when their teaching was impactful and effective, they couldn't always articulate why they were using the strategies they had chosen. She felt confident in the teaching abilities of her faculty, but felt they could be even more effective if they understood the science of learning and map effective teaching strategies onto it.

The previous summer, she had ordered several books and downloaded several resources to get an overview of existing research. Together with her instructional coaches and focus groups of teachers, they chose an instructional design model that made the most sense for their needs. They kicked off the year by providing an overview of the various models they had reviewed and the rationale for choosing the one they did. They "unpacked" the instructional design model, identifying appropriate teaching strategies for each phase of learning, scheduled regular "bite-sized" professional learning sessions throughout the year to dig more deeply into a few key strategies, and then organized peer observations and created learning communities to help teachers hone their use of the strategies in their classroom.

With the faculty, they identified measures of success to which they would hold themselves accountable. By mid-winter, Julia and her leadership team were seeing vast improvements in instruction. She overheard teachers discussing their instruction in ways that were more reflective and evidence-based than before. Best of all, she began seeing improvement in her students as they benefited from the well-designed lessons and units that teachers were delivering.

As she reflects on her school's success to date, Julia jots down some ideas for how to maintain momentum with the initiative: book chapters to read, discussions to have, and fun-yet-thoughtful activities to re-engage the faculty once everyone is back on campus in the fall. She feels buoyed by a sense of optimism that comes from having a plan, sticking to it, and seeing it bear fruit. ~

COMING OFF THE RAILS

Meanwhile, on the other side of the city, in a similarly sized school, Barbara is also reflecting on the previous year as she gazes out of her window and realizes she's biting her nails—a bad habit she can't seem to shake. She, too, launched an effort to implement an instructional design model at the beginning of the year. She had learned about the importance of instructional models the previous spring at a conference and came back convinced that one model in particular—the one promoted by a dynamic presenter at the conference—was the answer to her school's poor performance. She scheduled an intense week-long professional training for her faculty at the end of summer and brought in the best facilitators she could find. She was clear in her expectations for teachers: Every lesson plan and unit would follow the model, she and her leadership team would be in everyone's classrooms two or three times per week to ensure everyone was following the model, and a hefty chunk of teachers' performance evaluations would be tied to how consistently they employed the model in the classroom. *That ought to light a fire under everyone,* she had thought.

Within a few weeks of the start of the school, ordinary grumbling among teachers had erupted into defiance in faculty meetings. They wanted to know why she had chosen this particular model. They found flaws or counter-arguments to the research and used those to dismiss the body of work altogether. Those who did adopt the model seemed to do so out of compliance rather than enthusiasm for the work, which led to criticisms that the model was sucking the joy out of learning. She sensed many teachers were actively opposed to the very idea of an instructional model now. Some vocal parents (likely riled up by antagonistic teachers) also began questioning the model; Barbara's email inbox and voicemail had become increasingly filled with complaints and questions.

At the end of the year, she's unsure how to move forward. If she doubles down, she's likely to face more resistance, maybe even turning the few remaining teachers who appear to be in her corner against her. If she backs off, though, she fears that she'll appear weak or inconsistent in the face of adversity. She wonders how the whole effort came off the rails so quickly. Maybe, she thinks, she ought to just hang it up and see if another school in the district is looking for a new principal; perhaps she just needs to get away from her stubborn, naysaying teachers and find a place where teachers "get it"—where teachers actually want to get better. That thought, however, prompts her to recall some advice she'd recently given her own teenage daughter—about four fingers pointing back at us when we point fingers at others. *It's me*, she realizes with despair. *I really messed this up. What should I have done differently?*

IN THE SAME BOAT

In these two schools, teachers, too, are reflecting on the year and how they plan to move forward after a much-needed summer break.

Robert, a fourth-year teacher in Julia's school, is looking forward to his upcoming travels, but also feels energized to return in the fall to begin his new role as a mentor teacher. Before this year, he'd watched in frustration as he and his teammates struggled with certain students. They were a dedicated team, so they didn't want to write off under-performing students, yet they didn't have a roadmap for success. They often wrote their lesson plans in isolation and there were few opportunities for peer observation, feedback, or professional dialogue. Most teachers suffered alone in silence.

All of that changed when Julia had brought to a faculty meeting more than a year ago an article on the power of effective instructional design models. For Robert, it had been a watershed moment. For years, he'd been using what he'd learned in college to develop lesson plans—having a beginning, middle, end, and all of that. Yet he realized his planning had become somewhat perfunctory. It was also mostly focused on what he was doing as the teacher—not what students were doing, thinking, and learning. At the next faculty meeting, Julia invited professional dialogue about where people were currently when it came to instructional design and delivery. Quickly, it became evident that people's professional practices were all over the map. Some were meticulous planners. Some were basically winging it. Most seemed to agree a lesson or unit should have different parts, but there was less agreement about what those parts ought to be; they also had drastically different opinions about whether various strategies, like cooperative learning, were necessary. For Robert, who spent his summers in college waiting tables, it felt like he and his colleagues were running a restaurant in which every table got a different menu.

So, when Julia asked for volunteers to serve on a team to identify an instructional model for the school, Robert leapt at the chance. He and his colleagues spent a few weeks learning what instructional design models people were already using. At first some veteran teachers—including some widely regarded as the best in the school—insisted they weren't using any particular model, but rather, trusting their instincts as professionals. Yet as they explained how they guided student learning in the classroom, it became evident they **were** following a model—one that they had so deeply embedded into their practice they no longer thought about it. One remarked that maybe it was like playing jazz—she knew the song so well she could improvise and "riff" off her students.

Robert and his colleagues then set about identifying various instructional design models and considering which current models seemed to be the best fit for the challenges their students were facing. Watching the power of professionals coming together was career-changing for Robert. He started volunteering to lead book discussions, eagerly attended a few Saturday training sessions, and noted with pride that his and his teammates' efforts began to pay off for their students. Julia also noticed his growth and on the last day of classes, asked him to consider becoming a mentor teacher in the coming year. He accepted enthusiastically, thrilled that his four years of dedication to his profession was beginning to provide leadership opportunities. ~

RUNAWAY TRAIN

Meanwhile, on the other side of town, as summer rolls around, Robert's friend, Angela, also a fourth-year teacher, can't wait to put school in her rear-view mirror, spend some time at her parents' fishing cabin, and decompress after a difficult year at Barbara's school. She's never felt so frustrated and disengaged as a teacher. At first, with some caution, she embraced the new instructional model. It seemed sensible enough. Yet conversations quickly derailed during faculty meetings.

Some faculty were angry they hadn't been a part of the decision-making. Others had read critiques of the model and made up their minds early on that this shift was a huge mistake. In the faculty lounge, teachers clearly resented the intrusion of Barbara and her leadership team in their classrooms to check up on them—"treating us like children," as one teacher said. Another complained that she'd received several "nasty-grams" after Barbara's classroom visits, presumably because she wasn't using the model in her lessons. "I don't need to follow some stupid model. I mean, maybe if I were fresh out of school it would be fine, but I've got a master's degree; I know a thing or two about how to teach kids, thank you very much," she groused.

As much as she wanted to support Barbara and be a team player, Angela found herself struggling to implement the model in her classroom; she worried her teaching was becoming too formulaic and stale—that she might be "think-pair-sharing" her kids to death, but didn't have any good alternatives to help them process their learning. Yet already the detractors in the school seemed to resent her visibly trying to apply the model in her classroom, so she worried if she turned to her colleagues for simple advice, feedback, or brainstorming, they'd see through her questions and label her a "brown noser." So, she suffered alone.

The detractors' negative attitudes about the instructional model also seemed to be rubbing off on students—as became evident one day when a student asked, impertinently, "Are you going to make us do that I-do, we-do, you-do stuff again?" Only he hadn't used the word *stuff,* so she'd had to send him to the principal's office.

She suspects conversations are going on without her—that some of the teachers are plotting against Barbara. She sees the bags under Barbara's eyes and knows her principal could use her support now, but as one of the newer members of the faculty, is afraid to speak up at meetings. Right now, it feels as if the whole school has become a runaway train, barreling down a mountain with a bridge out ahead. Thus, she's relieved to have a summer break to hop off the train, so to speak, and get away from the dysfunction. She feels bad for

Barbara, yet feels she's at a loss for how to help her—or whether it's even possible to salvage the situation. *Maybe*, she tells herself, *I'll see if there are any openings at Robert's school. He seems to love it there.*

Can the successful use of an instructional design model really mean the difference between hating or loving where you work? Not to over-promise or anything, but yes, we think it can. We'll check in again with these characters as you begin to envision how a model can change the life of your school—and everyone in it.

Chapter 3: Choosing the right model for you

Consider in the last chapter how Barbara enthusiastically brought in an instructional model she had learned about at a conference and, with the best of intentions, began to implement the model the following school year. Without buy-in from your faculty or a clear understanding of why you've chosen a particular model, your initiative has little chance of being successful. Unfortunately, this is a mistake we see happen often. While the time commitment to getting faculty on board can seem counterproductive, it is crucial to build understanding and momentum before diving into a new initiative.

It's an overused sentiment, but still applicable: "There is no silver bullet." There is no *one* instructional model that solves all problems or is capable of being useful in every situation. To select the model that best suits the specific needs of your organization, we recommend that you first conduct a needs assessment to analyze where your faculty could use the most support and alignment or where your students seem to struggle the most.

Create a research and innovation team to guide your needs assessment

In *Curiosity Works: A Guidebook for Moving Your School from Improvement to Innovation* (2018), Goodwin, Rouleau, and Lewis encourage schools to create a Research and Innovation (R&I) Team—a group of leaders from across your school who help you stay focused on, and committed to, your improvement efforts. We recommend a similar group to conduct your needs assessment and frame your entire effort to implement an instructional model as an "R&D" effort—akin to how high-tech companies engage in rapid-cycle improvement to identify, develop, test, and improve products.

When bringing this team together, you'll want to ensure they represent your entire school in important ways—across grade levels, subject areas, specialty areas, and experience. Also, consider attitudes and dispositions. This work isn't easy, so it's important to have a team of people who ask hard questions, yet in the end, seek to accentuate the positive, lead by example, and create a collective sense of can-do optimism.

Size up the situation to ensure you're solving the *right* problem

You've likely picked up this book (and made it this far in reading it) because you're convinced—or at least pretty sure—that getting an instructional model in place will help improve achievement in your school. That's great. Nonetheless, we're all prone to confirmation bias (seeing what we want to see or are looking to find) at times, so let's make certain that an instructional model is actually the right solution for your problem—and doesn't become a solution in search of a problem.

To do that, we strongly recommend (if you haven't already done so) that you take a snapshot of the current state of instruction in your school or district by conducting a thorough needs assessment, which should include at least two (and ideally more) sources of data, including (but not limited to) the following:

- formative and summative assessment data from teachers
- classroom observations, walkthroughs, or instructional rounds
- interviews or focus groups with students, teachers, and parents
- surveys with students, teachers, and parents
- standardized achievement data

Essentially, you want to understand the current "state of play" in your school when it comes to classroom instruction. As you review these data, you might consider the following questions:

- Do you see consistent, high-quality instruction in every classroom . . . or more of a "box of chocolates" (you never know what you're gonna get from one classroom to the next)?
- What great practices (or "bright spots") do you see that you might want to be sure to include in your instructional model? What "best practices" are already in place?
- Do teachers already appear to be following an instructional model?
- Can teachers articulate *why* they're doing *what* they're doing in their classrooms? That is, can they articulate a "theory of action" or "mental model" that guides how they design learning experiences for students?
- What do *students* say about their learning experiences? Do they find them to be challenging? Engaging?
- What patterns do you see in student achievement data? Is there classroom-level variance in achievement—are students performing significantly better in some classrooms than others?
- Can you attribute those differences to what you've observed in classrooms?

Take a closer look with instructional rounds

We cannot overemphasize the value of engaging in a series of instructional rounds to help you get a handle on what instruction currently looks like in classrooms (see below for more specific guidance on instructional rounds if you're not already familiar with the process). As you observe classrooms, we encourage you to view them through a lens of asset-based thinking—looking for the great things that are already happening in your school that you'd like to see become consistent, regular practice in all classrooms (Goodwin et al., 2018).

> ### What are instructional rounds?
>
> Instructional rounds are brief (10–15 minute) observations of classrooms focused on teaching and learning.
>
> Typically, a small group (2–3 people) visit a rotation of classes to gather descriptive (not evaluative) evidence of what they see occurring in classrooms.
>
> Avoid using rubrics or scoring sheets. Instead, simply make mental or written notes about questions and positives you see. You can use the questions below as starters.
>
> - What bright spots are occurring?
> - How consistently do we see these bright spots happening?
> - When students appear challenged and engaged, what activities are they doing?
> - What classroom conditions are present?
> - What are teachers doing?
> - What might it look like if the bright spots occurred in every classroom?
>
> Afterward, the groups share their observations, reflecting on and sharing "bright spots" and best practices—things that worked well in one classroom that could be applied or adapted in others.

Use Tool 1 on p. 31 to record your notes and guide your post-observation reflection with fellow teachers.

Starting the process by simply observing (without judgment) what's already *going right* in classrooms is important for a few reasons. For starters, you might discover that most teachers *are already* using an instructional design model in their classrooms and spare yourself (and them) from the headache of over-correcting a problem that's mostly solved. It's quite likely, though, that you'll see some inconsistencies—great practices that aren't yet *common* practice. By being able to identify these practices first, you'll be in a better position to frame your effort to identify and adopt an instructional model as a means to accentuate the positive in your school—capturing and building on what's already working. In other words, instead of saying (or being perceived as saying), *You're doing it all wrong, now start doing it right*, you'll be able to say, *We're doing a lot of things right—this new instructional model will help us capture those things so that we can do them more consistently and thoughtfully,* which is, of course, a much more palatable message.

Connect observational data and student data

After you've conducted your instructional rounds, step back for a moment to consider connections between what you've seen in classrooms and student performance data. As an R&I Team, review assessment data and any information you have collected from students, parents, and staff through conversations, focus groups, and surveys. Use Tool 2 on pp. 32–33 to discuss and summarize your observations and conversations.

For example, these data might reveal that a certain group of students are progressing more slowly than their peers; high-achievers are doing well and students with learning differences are also showing good progress, but a "middle" group seems to be struggling on common formative assessments. So, as a team, you might decide to conduct even more focused classroom observations and invite teachers into professional dialogues during faculty meetings. During these observations and conversations, you may notice that many students are disengaged—they're uninterested from the outset of the lesson and claim confusion as the lesson progresses, sometimes saying, "I don't get it." They then seem to give up even though the material is within their reach. What could be happening?

As you reflect on your classroom observations, you might conclude that too many lessons are almost entirely whole-group instruction; during these lessons, students interact with teachers in something of an 80:20 ratio—20% of students do 80% of the talking in the classroom. As a result, most students go through an entire class period without speaking a word or making their thinking visible—*to anyone*, their teachers or peers. Meanwhile, you may have noticed classrooms where most, if not all, students are engaged in regular conversations about their learning. A deeper dive into the performance data reveals that in these classrooms there is no forgotten middle—all students are performing at higher levels. Thus, you may conclude that any model you choose needs to support student talk in the classroom, providing them with opportunities to make their thinking visible with peers and teachers.

Assess teachers' current knowledge and use of instructional design models

Once you've compiled a snapshot of instructional practices in your classrooms, as an R&I Team, you'll likely want to engage in follow-up conversations with teachers (as individuals or in small groups) to explore their current familiarity with and/or use of instructional models. For example, you might want to ask them the following questions:

- Do you follow a model for instructional design? If so, which one?
- How do you decide which instructional strategies to incorporate into a lesson?
- What fundamental understandings of how students learn do you follow when designing learning opportunities for students (e.g., massed practice accelerates learning while distributed practice supports retention)?
- If you follow an instructional model, do you feel you have a broad repertoire of instructional strategies and learning activities to incorporate into your lesson and unit designs?

As a group, you'll want to assess, in a general sense, teachers' current use of instructional design models. You might do this by considering which of the following descriptors most closely reflect your schools' use of instructional models and/or use these descriptors to develop one for your own school or school system.

Table 2. Draft rubric for considering current use of instructional models

Idiosyncratic	Partial or mixed	Perfunctory	Intentional
A few of our teachers use an instructional design model, but most do not. Many seem to sequence learning activities with little reflection on why they're selecting particular teaching strategies or tasks.	Our teachers are supposed to use an instructional model to design learning, yet many do not—or use a different model than colleagues. As a result, we seem to be speaking "different languages" when it comes to instruction.	Our teachers mostly follow the same instructional model, but in rigid, simplistic, or disengaging ways (e.g., relying too much on a particular strategy or overdoing particular parts of the model).	Our teachers have internalized the learning model and use it to reflect on student learning, engage in professional dialogue, diagnose learning challenges, and share lesson ideas with one another.

The judgments you make here—how you size up your current reality—will shape your next step. If, for example, you don't detect any particular model already in use in your school, you may wish to start from scratch by looking for a model that aligns with your own philosophies of learning, staff capabilities, and the needs of your students. But if you observe that many teachers already are following a similar model and experiencing success with it, you may simply wish to scale-up use of that model. Alternatively, if you've seen a hodgepodge of models in use, you may wish to synthesize current practice into a model of your own (which we'll help you think through in the following section). Or you may find that teachers have become too rigid with a particular model (e.g., "think-pair-sharing" the daylights out of students or employing a particular learning sequence like "I-do-we-do-you-do" ad nauseum) and thus, decide you need to refresh the model or help teachers better understand the science of learning—the *why* behind the *what*.

Involve teachers in the process

While your R&I Team should continue to guide the process of choosing a model, it's a good idea to broaden the process to a larger group of stakeholders as you begin to review various models to see which one may be the best fit in your school. Doing so will not only help to increase buy-in to the overall process, but also help to surface which instructional design models teachers are already using or feel most comfortable following.

Engaging teachers in the process can also help you avoid over-solving a problem (and creating a new one) if they're already following a model but see some simple, yet significant ways to improve it. For example, if you've found students are disengaged in most classrooms, shared inquiry among teachers of other instructional design models might lead everyone to conclude that the current instructional design model generally works well, yet needs to be enhanced with a more explicit focus on engaging student interest at the beginning of lessons and units as well as "chunking" learning so students have time to consolidate and reflect on new knowledge. As a result, your R&I Team might decide to modify your lesson plan template to list possible activities that teachers can use to make these enhancements and ask teachers to note which ones work best. Through this process, your teachers might agree together to set up "learning stations" that include didactic manipulatives, reflection opportunities, and drawing and other visual sense-making activities to help students grasp concepts and make their thinking visible.

Adopt, adapt, or develop a model of instruction?

As you and your R&I Team colleagues dig into instructional design models, you'll quickly discover there's a myriad of models from which to choose. That's the bad news. The good news is that most models tend to reflect similar approaches to sequencing learning. In Table 3, we offer a side-by-side comparison of several of the most common models, mapping them onto a common set of phases of learning. At a high level, most of these reflect similar approaches to learning, with some differences in terms of granularity and terminology that can, in turn, point to some important differences in pedagogical principles. Some models (e.g., Engelmann's Direct Instruction) arguably reflect more teacher-led, didactic approaches to instruction while others (e.g., Kolb's Experiential Model) reflect a more student-centered, constructivist approach to learning, and still others (e.g., Explicit Direct Instruction) are more of a blend of these two approaches—often starting with teacher-led instruction followed by learner-directed independent practice and experimentation.

We encourage you to explore each of these models in more depth (see pp. 24–25). As you explore these models and consider which makes the most sense for your school and your students, we'd encourage you to reflect on the "bright spots" in teacher practice that you observed in classrooms during your instructional rounds, considering how the practices you want to see occurring in more classrooms are reflected in these models. Examples might be the use of probing questions to guide learning, students working in collaborative groups to consolidate and reflect on learning, or students engaged in independent learning projects to apply new learning in novel situations. Making these connections explicit will help teachers see their own classrooms in the model you adopt, adapt, or develop.

Table 3. Synthesized list of instructional models

Stage or phase	5E Instructional Model *BSCS*	Direct Instruction *Engelmann*	Experiential Learning *Kolb*	Explicit Direct Instruction *Hollingsworth & Ybarra*
Engage interest	Engage	Introduce new concept/review prior learning		Activate prior knowledge
Set goals for learning				Learning objective
Guide new learning	Explore Explain	Present concept with examples/non-examples	Concrete experience Reflective observation	Concept development Skill development
Consolidate and reflect on learning	Elaborate	Student response Teacher feedback	Abstract conceptualization	Guided practice Relevance
Apply new learning	Evaluate	Independent practice	Active experimentation	Closure

Five Episodes of Instruction Silver & Strong	Gradual Release of Responsibility Fisher & Frey	Master Teaching Hunter	New Teacher's Companion Cunningham	Nine Events of Instruction Gagné	Student Learning That Works McREL
Prepare students for new learning		Anticipatory set	Introduction	Gaining attention	Become interested
	Focus lesson	Objective and purpose	Foundation	Informing the learner of the objective	Commit to learning
Presenting new learning	Guided instruction ("I do")	Input Modeling	Brain activation Body of new information	Stimulating recall of prerequisite learning Presenting the stimulus material Providing learning guidance	Focus on new learning
Deepening and reinforcing learning	Productive group work Guided instruction ("We do")	Checking for understanding Guided practice	Clarification Practice and review	Eliciting the performance Providing feedback Assessing the performance	Make sense of learning Rehearse and reflect
Applying learning Reflecting on and celebrating learning	Independent learning ("You do")	Independent practice Closure	Independent practice Closure	Enhancing retention and transfer	Extend and apply

Recall your ultimate goal here: to provide teachers with concrete guidance, clarity, and common vocabulary for instructional design to help them deliver *consistent,* high-quality instruction in every classroom. So, in a way, which model you choose may be less important than picking a model and sticking with it. Here, you have three options:

- **Adopt a model**. This is a sensible option if a) you have limited time, energy, resources, or capacity to develop your own model, b) a particular model strongly aligns with your team's philosophy of teaching and learning, c) it's important for you to select a tried-and-true model with existing resources (lesson plans, professional learning, and the like), or d) a majority (or plurality) of your teachers are already using a particular model and having success with it, so you'll get farther faster by encouraging schoolwide use of a model that many teachers are already happily using. Perhaps the biggest advantage to adopting an existing model is that you may be able to move more quickly, leverage the credibility of an existing research base, and support your teachers with more "off-the-shelf" resources; disadvantages could include that teachers, especially more-experienced ones, might resist an external program especially if they don't feel it reflects their current practice or understanding of what good teaching looks like in the classroom.

- **Adapt a model**. You might go this route if an existing model *mostly* aligns with your philosophy of teaching and learning but could be better aligned with some key enhancements (e.g., grafting independent project-based learning activities onto an otherwise teacher-led approach). Or you might determine that an existing model resonates with your team *in principle* but in practice, uses a different set of vocabulary than your teachers have been using or may have learned through prior professional learning (e.g., referring to an "anticipatory set" versus a "hook," etc.). Thus, you might choose to follow the model, but switch out some language for more familiar terms. Finally, you might find that teachers have been using different models that could be integrated together into an even more robust or effective approach—something of a "chocolate and peanut butter" solution. The advantages of *adapting* a model are leveraging existing resources, aligning the model with prior efforts and professional learning, and demonstrating that you've been listening to teachers and aren't simply adopting an external solution wholesale. Disadvantages can include creating a "Frankenstein" solution that looks good in theory, but becomes unworkable in practice; you may also find that you're constantly needing to retrofit existing resources into your new model.

- **Develop a model**. As you dig into existing models, you may see bits and pieces you like about many of them. You may also find, as an R&I Team, that the process of inquiry—of researching, reflecting, and engaging teacher input—has become a tremendously powerful learning opportunity, one that you want others to benefit from experiencing. So, you may decide to develop your own model, one that you can dub the [name of your school/district] Model of Learning. The advantages of creating your own include stakeholder engagement—teachers will be more apt to see themselves, their current practice, and expertise reflected in the model. Moreover, your entire school or district team may benefit from a deep dive into the science of learning and instructional design that the process requires. Disadvantages can include moving more slowly than with the other two approaches to ensure you develop a thoughtful approach; also, if you seek to include everyone's opinion you may wind up creating a hyper-complicated model (akin to Mark Twain's quip about a camel being a horse designed by committee). Finally, as you'll also need to develop your own resources, including model lessons and professional learning, you'll want to consider if you have the time, resources, and staff capacity to do all of that.

> **Creating your own model: A Texas example**
>
> In an effort to ensure all students experienced engaging, yet challenging learning opportunities in every classroom, Fort Worth Independent School District (ISD) developed their own model of learning, one that reflects an inquiry-driven approach to learning. You can learn more about the Fort Worth ISD model at https://www.fwisd.org/Page/14281.

Being transparent with your decisions

Regardless of which approach you take, you should consider in advance—and clearly communicate to all stakeholders—how you'll make these decisions, including what criteria you'll use to evaluate different models or approaches and who will make the ultimate decision.

Clarifying review criteria

For starters, you should consider your selection criteria. How important is it that the model be based on research or have demonstrated evidence of impact? How important is it that it reflects what's already working well in your classrooms (your "bright spots")? How important is it that it accesses readily available resources to support implementation of the model? Are you seeking a model that provides *general principles* of instructional design or a more detailed (i.e., step-by-step) process for teachers to follow? How important is it that the model reflects shared ideals and beliefs about student learning (e.g., should it be student-centered, culturally appropriate, etc.)? What are those ideals and beliefs?

In the tools for this chapter, we provide a sample review rubric (see Tool 3 on page 34) for you to adapt in creating your own model. After reviewing several models using your established criteria, you may find one that meets most or all of your needs. Or realize that you'd like to adapt a model or determine that creating your own model—perhaps synthesizing from those you've been reviewing—is the best path forward.

Communicating how decisions will be made

Before engaging in this process, you should communicate with everyone how the final decision will be made. Will the R&I Team make the final call? Or will the principal have the final say? Will it be by vote with majority rule? It won't help your cause if your faculty thinks the majority will have the final say when, in actuality it will be the R&I Team. By anticipating these questions and being upfront about how the decisions will be made, you increase your chances of getting faculty on board, even if their preferred framework isn't chosen. Your success in implementing an instructional model with consistency is likely to hinge on how well you've articulated how the choice was made. Having data to back up your decision is key—including the criteria you used to select it and how other models stacked up against one another on those criteria. Regardless of how you make your decision, you should be transparent and upfront about how it will be made. In other words, don't ask for faculty input or give the expectation that the majority will rule if, in fact, the decision will be made by you and/or your team.

Ideally, you should have no more than six people involved in making decisions as you go through your change implementation (Larson, 2017). While teams generally outperform single leaders, having too much input can result in inertia stemming from ineffective debate. Consider the following options on p. 29 and decide what will work best for you and your team as you come to major decisions in implementing your model.

Table 4. Methods for decision making

Method	Definition	Pros	Cons
Command	Leader makes decision without input.	Efficiency	Lack of input can result in resistance, ineffective implementation, or revolt. Decisions may also lack key information and perspectives that could help the change be successful.
Input followed by command	Leader gets input, but ultimately makes the final decision.	Efficiency, opportunity for leader to gather key information and perspectives	Those who give input but feel their advice is not followed may feel the request for input was simply to "save face."
Consensus	100% of the group must agree.	Very good chance of buy-in and implementation since team members feel heard	Reaching this level of agreement can be extremely time-consuming or result in compromise solutions that ultimately satisfy no one.
Solid Majority	At least 60% of the group must agree.	Better chance of buy-in since team members feel heard	Reaching this level of consensus can take longer as you discuss, gather information and perspectives, and debate.
Majority	More than 50% of the group must agree.	Better chance of buy-in since team members feel heard	There is a chance that almost half of those who voted will have to implement something for which they did not vote.

Final reflection and checklist

Before you move onto the next phase of the process, rolling out the model to teachers, take a moment as an R&I Team to consider the following questions about your teachers, your school culture, and your readiness for this change. We've also provided a checklist to confirm you've addressed all of the important tasks at this stage in the process.

Reflecting together

As an R&I Team, ask yourselves the following questions:

1. Where, in our school, are we seeing the greatest success right now? Where are students most engaged and enthusiastic? Which areas seem to have the biggest impact on student growth? Have we celebrated these with teachers?

2. What mechanisms do we currently have in place for gathering data on student learning? Have we made connections between positive outcomes and teacher practice?

3. What mechanisms do we currently have in place for instructional leaders and teachers to observe and learn from one another? How comfortable are we with having others observe our practice?

4. What practices do I currently have in place to give teachers a safe space to share what they are doing in their classrooms, what impact it had, and what challenges they're encountering in order to receive feedback from peers?

Checklist for choosing the right model for your school

- ☐ Create a Research and Innovation (R&I) Team to guide the process.
- ☐ Conduct instructional rounds and reflect on bright spots, using Tools 1 and 2.
- ☐ Create a snapshot of current practice and needs.
- ☐ Develop review criteria for evaluating instructional models, using Tool 3.
- ☐ Clarify and communicate decision making.
- ☐ Explore instructional models.
- ☐ Select a model to adopt, adapt, or develop.

Check out
Chapter 3 Tools
on the following pages

Tool 1: Using instructional rounds to find bright spots

After you have completed an instructional rounds cycle, record the following information.

Focus of visit:

Observers' comments about:

- **Affirmations** (strategies to keep using):

- **Reflections** (strategies to reconsider):

- **Considerations** (strategies you'd like to try):

What conditions did the team identify as necessary to replicate (and potentially scale) the bright spots?

What five key messages about your school—its challenges and bright spots—should everyone in your community know?

1. _____.

2. _____.

3. _____.

4. _____.

5. _____.

Source: *Curiosity Works: A Guidebook for Moving Your School from Improvement to Innovation*. McREL 2018.

Tool 2: Connecting observational data and student data

	Formative and summative assessment data from teachers	Classroom observations, walkthroughs, or instructional rounds
What are the bright spots?		
When students are challenged and engaged, what are they doing?		
What classroom conditions are present?		
What are teachers doing?		
How consistently do we see these bright spots?		
What might it look like if they were present in every classroom?		

Interviews or focus groups with students, teachers, and parents	Surveys with students, teachers, and parents	Standardized achievement data

Tool 3: Sample rubric for evaluating instructional models

Review criteria	No (1)	Somewhat (2)	Yes (3)	Weighting *How important is this to us?*
Is the model supported with a strong research base?		2		25%
Does the model reflect our bright spots?	1			15%
Are resources available to support implementation?	1			10%
Is the model clear, intuitive, and simple to follow?		2		20%
Does it support student-centered learning?			3	30%

Chapter 4: Planning for successful professional learning

Now that you've chosen your instructional design model, the real work begins: helping teachers use the model effectively in their classrooms to ensure consistent, high-quality instruction, which after all, is the driving purpose of this entire effort. In our fictional example at the beginning of this book, Barbara, whose efforts to implement an instructional model in her school came off the rails, wrongly assumed her teachers would be able to use the model consistently in their classrooms after attending an intensive professional learning conference with a high-priced consultant. What Barbara failed to consider is the vexing challenge of the so-called knowing-doing gap—that simply *knowing* better doesn't always translate into *doing* better. Often, that's because what lies between knowing and doing is a change in habits; as a result, school change often requires *many individuals* to change *many habits* at once—no small feat, indeed.

In this chapter, we'll help you to prepare for this complex undertaking by considering how to support your teachers by providing them with effective *professional learning* (helping them to *know* better) as well as creating opportunities for them to receive feedback, reflect, and improve their practices (helping them to *do* better as well).

Start with moral purpose

Regardless of which model you've decided to implement, you'll want to start by helping teachers understand the deeper purpose for implementing an instructional model in their classrooms. Consider what Simon Sinek observed in his 2009 TED Talk and 2011 book *Start with Why*: "People don't buy what you do, they buy *why* you do it." That is, people are more apt to embrace a challenge when it connects to their emotions and deeper sense of purpose. Chip and Dan Heath (2010) noted something similar in their book, *Switch: How to Change Things When Change is Hard*—namely, despite what we might tell ourselves, feelings and emotions are far more powerful drivers of behavior than cool-headed logic, facts, or research studies. If anything, we tend to use reasoning, logic, and statistics to justify what our emotions and instincts have already told us to do.

So, as you think about rolling out your instructional model, we urge you to pause a moment and consider as an R&I Team *why* you are doing this. Hopefully, your answer goes deeper than just trying to improve your test scores or get someone in a central office or state capitol off your back. Ideally, you should be able to draw a solid line from your own *why* as a professional—that is, *why* you got into this line of work (or as some would say, heeded the calling) of education in the first place. So, before plunging right into a slew of workshops, take some time to ask yourself the following questions as a leadership team—and ultimately, as an entire school faculty. Ask everyone to share:

1. Why are you an educator? What drew you into the profession? And what keeps you here?

2. How do you want your students to remember you? What adjectives would you want them to use when they describe you years or decades from now?

3. In what ways could implementing an instructional model consistently in our classrooms help us to achieve our purpose and leave a legacy as educators?

These questions are important to ask because research finds that people are more apt to change their practice when they see themselves as part of a team working together to accomplish something bigger than themselves. So, by articulating and sharing these ideas with one another, you'll have something you can return to, reminding yourselves of what you're really trying to accomplish when the going gets tough (and it will) so that, collectively, you're able to pull together and stay the course.

Generate interest and enthusiasm with a kickoff event

Now that you've started with *why*, it's time to consider *how* you'll support teacher learning. Here, you'll want to plan a well-orchestrated kickoff event, one that speaks to your teachers' minds *and hearts*, helping them to understand the "bright spots" and opportunities for growth you've seen in classrooms as well as what surfaced in student data—and makes clear how the instructional model will help to build on these bright spots and support everyone's growth as professionals. Also, you'll want to remind everyone of the process you used to identify the learning model you've adopted, adapted, or developed. Most importantly (so important, in fact, you might want to start with it) you'll want to show that the model reflects your shared moral purpose as a school or district—be it changing kids' lives, igniting their passions and interests, or ensuring their success as future citizens and leaders.

The most obvious times to launch a new initiative are at the beginning of the school year or the start of summer, as that's a time that many teachers spend planning new lessons. While we have seen successful implementations start midyear, we find the energy and enthusiasm necessary to engage in new learning is at its peak as faculty returns from summer break. Most of us tend to associate back-to-school time as an opportunity for fresh starts and new beginnings, so we tend to be more willing to try something new at the start of a school year than once the year has begun. To build excitement for the new model, you might consider giving teachers a "sneak peek" into the new model by providing them with advance copies of the book or manual you plan to use—as elective, not assigned, reading—to encourage buy-in.

As you plan your kickoff event, consider how you will apply the new model to your teacher learning activities. For example, if you're using a model that begins with "hooking" student interest (as many models do), your professional learning session should do the same, using a "hook" or "anticipatory set" (or whatever terminology your chosen model employs) to grab teacher interest in the day's learning. Similarly, you'll want to engage teachers in other phases of learning reflected in the model *as they learn about it*. After all, what better way is there to learn about an instructional design model than to experience it for ourselves? While this may seem obvious, we've seen a great deal of adult learning that seems to throw everything we know about the science of learning out the window—which applies to adults as well as to kids. So, don't miss the opportunity to model (as it were) your new model for teachers.

Most likely, you'll want your kickoff session to provide an overview of the model, giving teachers an opportunity to dive into it and consider how to apply it in their classrooms. For this, you might encourage teachers to bring an existing lesson and/or unit plan to redesign using the new model so that, shortly after the kickoff session, they can begin experimenting with and implementing the model in their classrooms. (Doing so will also likely reflect your chosen instructional design model, as most conclude with a phase for applied learning, independent practice, transfer, experimentation, or the like).

Even though instructional design is a lot to absorb, it's best to keep your kickoff sessions short and focused. We recommend no more than a single day, and even that's a long stretch unless it's a true workshop with lots of opportunities for teachers to work together to process how to apply the model in their lesson plans and classroom activities. Bear in mind, most of the teachers' *real learning* doesn't actually happen during the workshop itself, but rather, afterward, as they apply the model in their classrooms and reflect on what's working, what's not, and what adjustments they need to make.

Develop goals for learning and classroom application

With all of this in mind, be sure to share upfront your shared goals for the professional learning—both during and after the session. Here again, you should apply the same terminology as your instructional model (i.e., framing "goals," "objectives," "success criteria," or the like in the same way you want teachers to do for students). We'd also encourage you to apply the principles of S.M.A.R.T. (Specific, Measurable, Achievable, Relevant, and Time-bound) goals when defining these outcomes. For example, you might define a shared goal following the first professional learning session for teachers to develop and deliver a six-week unit of study that employs the learning model. In a subsequent session—say, a deeper dive into setting and sharing student learning objectives and success criteria—you might set a goal of every teacher being able to successfully and consistently articulate success criteria at the beginning of the lesson and for students to be able to articulate to a neighbor (or classroom observer) what they should know or be able to do at the end of the lesson.

Create benchmarks to track your progress

Your next step as a group will be to agree upon benchmarks. Where do you expect to be by the end of the semester? By the end of the school year? Here, we encourage you to consider using an innovation configuration map to clarify for teachers what it should look like to use the instructional model in their classrooms.

> ## What is an innovation configuration map?
> An innovation configuration (IC) map describes how the key elements of a program, practice, or change initiative (an innovation) looks along a continuum from low- to high-level implementation. When collaboratively developed, an IC map reflects a group's shared expectations about successful implementation of a new initiative, such as an instructional model, and thus provides a tool for teacher and leader reflection, feedback, and support throughout the implementation process.

Ideally, you could engage teachers in a collaborative process for developing these rubrics. In our experience, engaging teachers in this process not only increases buy-in, but also often results in teachers challenging one another to implement new changes with greater depth and consistency than principals or school leadership teams might otherwise have imposed upon them. Briefly, here's how the process works:

1. **Identify the key components of the instructional model.** Most likely, this will be the various stages of your model—from lesson launch to closure.

2. **Describe each component on a continuum from low- to high-level use.** Start by defining the "ideal," followed by "unacceptable," and then the incremental stages in between. For example, you might define *ideal* use of the "learning objective" component of your instructional model as "Engaging students in developing personal goals for units and connecting lesson objectives to unit goals" and *unacceptable* as "Failing to display or articulate learning objectives for lessons or units."

3. **Focus on describing, not rating, behaviors.** IC maps differ from rubrics in that they simply *describe*, in a clear and tangible way, the level of use of a new practice, rather than *evaluate* behaviors. In short, your descriptors should be *observable* (e.g., *Can we see objectives in the classroom or hear teachers articulate them?*), rather than *subjective* (e.g., *Teachers do a good job providing learning objectives*).

4. **Arrange your columns from left to right, starting with "ideal."** This may feel a bit backwards, but it's intentional as it makes the ideal most prominent to readers—focusing them first on positive instead of negative.

See Tool 6 on p. 54 for an example and more information on creating IC maps.

As an R&I Team, you want to balance setting realistic goals with those that stretch people, helping them to envision new possibilities and inspiring them to achieve more for themselves and their students than they might originally have thought possible. That said, implementation often unfolds in fits and starts, so it's important to have benchmarks along the way, so you can show (and celebrate) progress as teachers are learning and refining new skills.

For example, teachers might commit to ensuring that learning objectives are visible and articulated for every lesson, and that students can articulate their objectives. Initially, classroom observations might reveal that learning objectives are visible in just 60% of classroom visits, but over a six-week period, this number increases to 95%. Moreover, when asked, 8 in 10 students can articulate these objectives clearly. Such change would be cause for celebration—one that would likely create a sense of positive momentum in the overall change initiative that might inspire more teachers to move closer to the ideal use of learning objectives in their classrooms. In chapter 6, we will spend more time discussing measuring progress toward success. This is where you will fine-tune your assessment protocols as you get deeper into the implementation phase.

Develop an approach to professional learning

Now that you're clear about where you're going, let's consider how you'll get there—how you'll facilitate teachers' professional learning to support their effective use of the instructional model in their classrooms. Here you have a number of options, each with its unique advantages and disadvantages. Let's consider each briefly.

- **Hire a consultant**. This might be a good way to kick off the school year, especially if you are *adopting* a model and feel having an "outside voice" will have more impact. You can also generally be assured that the consultant is steeped in the content and can deliver an engaging, informative session along with support materials and tools to assist in later implementation of the model. However, consultants are typically the most expensive option, especially if your school tends to have a high turnover rate and you anticipate needing to provide "refresher" training each year to a new group of teachers. Also, some external trainers may insist on fidelity to their particular model and would thus be unwilling to entertain changes to it, so this may be a less viable option if you plan to *adapt* a given model.

- **Train-the-trainer**. Sending instructional leaders to a training-of-trainer course or certification has its advantages. First, it can help you to develop in-house capacity and sustainability. Second, it can also allow your team to *adapt* a particular model with terminology more familiar to your teachers and/or enhancements that reflect your own shared agreements about your ideal approach to student learning. Third, teachers may respond better to "one of their own" sharing new ideas with them. Such training can still be costly, though, and rely on the comfort and skill level of your internal team to learn and teach the process with fidelity and resonate with teachers when delivering the content. We recommend you consider including influencers in your building(s) to serve as trainers, including those who don't necessarily have positional authority yet command respect and trust among their colleagues.

- **Collaborative inquiry**. This option engages professional learning communities in diving into externally or internally produced resources to learn about the model, apply it in classrooms, seek peer feedback, and coach one another to deliver the model with increasing precisions. Often, a DIY (do-it-yourself) approach is the most cost-effective option to implementing a new model. However, it can sometimes lack the insights or motivational qualities of an outside expert or internal team that has received in-depth training from an outside group. In short, you may get what you pay for. Nonetheless, this may be the most viable approach if a) you've developed your own model or b) you have well-established collegial learning communities who learn best when they learn together.

- **Focus on "early adopters."** A final approach that you can apply with any of the previous options is to focus your initial professional learning efforts on a small subset of teachers who have shown themselves most willing to learn (who lean in rather than sit with arms folded during professional learning sessions) and share the model with them, challenging them to serve as trailblazers in your school or district community. The benefit of creating a "coalition of the willing," so to speak, is that they're apt to move more quickly in embracing and incorporating the model into their classrooms and thus provide "vicarious experiences" from which later groups of teachers can draw inspiration and guidance when they apply the model. Also, your early adopters can work out some of the kinks in applying the model in your context, show others how the model works, and provide lesson plans and tips to assist in the transition process. In essence, you may find it more effective to "go slow to go fast" by focusing first on early adopters, who in turn can create positive peer influence (and a "tipping point") for more widespread later application of the model.

You can use Tool 4 on pp. 50–51 to consider your options and rank your criteria.

Supporting "precision without prescription" through peer coaching

Regardless of which approach you take, research is clear that professional learning rarely leads to sustained change in classroom practice without coaching. In fact, years ago, Joyce and Showers (2002) observed that describing the underlying theory of a new teaching practice, modeling its use, and providing teachers with opportunities to apply it in their own classrooms are all important, but only result in about 5% of teachers transferring new learning into their classrooms. When *peer coaching* was added as a component of professional learning, however, that number increased to 95% of teachers.

It's important to note that peer coaching can take two forms. One we might think of as *vertical* coaching: an expert advising a protégé. The second is *lateral* coaching: colleagues coaching one another. This latter form of true peer-to-peer coaching is what really ensures professional learning sticks in classrooms. However, studies have found that peer-to-peer coaching often fails for a couple of simple reasons. For starters, participants may not really know what the practice in question ought to look like in the classroom, so they're unsure what to look for or what pointers to give when observing a peer's classroom. In addition, teachers also tend to be so concerned with being nice to one another that they are reluctant to offer "critical friend" feedback. With this in mind, here are some ways to help teachers serve as effective peer-to-peer coaches:

- **Provide concrete descriptors of ideal practice.** This is where the innovation configuration maps you created earlier come in handy. Teachers can use them to objectively size up what they're seeing in colleagues' classrooms.
- **Invite feedback.** Teachers are more likely to give one another feedback when their peers *invite* the feedback by asking for specific pointers on particular aspects of their teaching that they're working to improve or have recently incorporated into their classrooms. For example, a teacher might ask a colleague to use a stopwatch to see if he's allowing three

or more seconds of "wait time" after posing a question and receiving responses from students. So, prior to peers observing their classrooms, teachers can volunteer areas where feedback would be most helpful.

- **Create peer coaching triads**. Another way to help teachers avoid "I'm OK, you're OK" platitudes is by encouraging them to work in teams of three, using the triad model described in Figure 1 below.

- **Remember, observers are also learners**. Finally, one of the biggest benefits to peer coaching is learning what others are doing; in other words, observers often learn as much as those they are observing, picking up new techniques and teaching strategies to use in their own classrooms. You can formalize this process by encouraging observers to identify things they will "borrow" in their own classrooms.

You can use Tool 7 on p. 55 and Tool 8 on p. 56 to create protocols for positive, productive observations and reflections.

Figure 1. Peer Coaching Triad

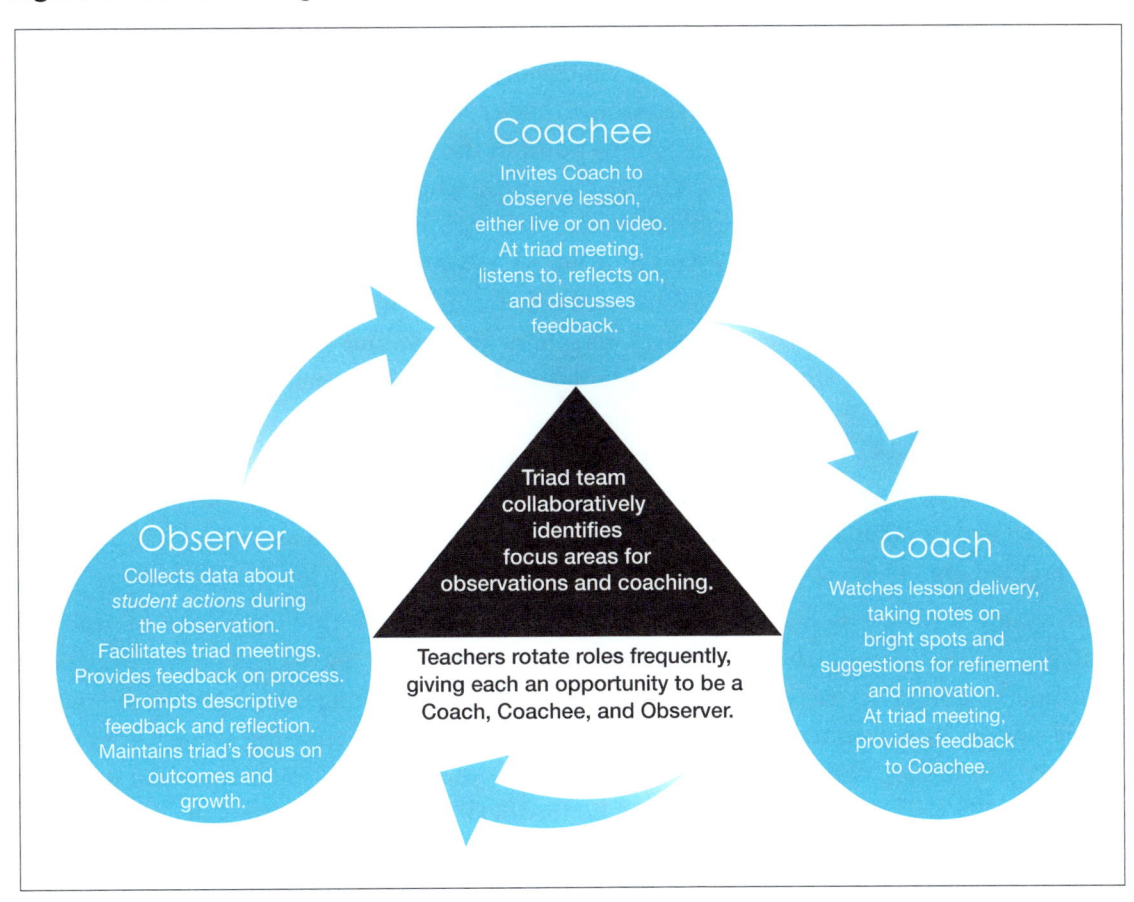

Coachee
Invites Coach to observe lesson, either live or on video. At triad meeting, listens to, reflects on, and discusses feedback.

Observer
Collects data about *student actions* during the observation. Facilitates triad meetings. Provides feedback on process. Prompts descriptive feedback and reflection. Maintains triad's focus on outcomes and growth.

Coach
Watches lesson delivery, taking notes on bright spots and suggestions for refinement and innovation. At triad meeting, provides feedback to Coachee.

Triad team collaboratively identifies focus areas for observations and coaching.

Teachers rotate roles frequently, giving each an opportunity to be a Coach, Coachee, and Observer.

Ideally, teachers will find time to observe one another's classrooms in person, even if for only a few minutes at a time during their own preparation period. However, if release time is an obstacle, you might also consider recording lessons, which can provide an added benefit of allowing teachers to rewind and take in everything that's happening in a peer's classroom.

Videos can also support observing classrooms in other schools or districts, which can be particularly helpful when teaching a unique subject area and/or in a remote location. Perhaps most important, remember to make it fun; peer observations are great opportunities for everyone to learn and grow. So, be sure to take time to celebrate the great things people are seeing and doing. Teaching, after all, can be a lonely, thankless profession with little outside affirmation of the tremendous efforts people put in every day to nurture young minds. As professionals, we need opportunities to share our handiwork—and receive the occasional pat on the back for a job well done.

Map out your professional learning schedule

Finally, you'll want to consider the cadence and frequency of formal professional learning opportunities for teachers over the course of the school year. Just as it's important for students to understand the arc or narrative of their learning—how each lesson connects with a larger unit—it's important for teachers to understand the various touchpoints of professional learning you will be providing for them. We encourage you to share your professional learning schedule and post it where faculty can easily access it. As we've already noted, implementing an instructional model is a complex endeavor, one that requires in-depth learning and extended opportunities for practice, feedback, and professional reflection. So, don't expect a magical, overnight transformation in every classroom in your school or district. More likely, you've embarked on a multi-year journey. So, at this point in the process, you'll want to consider how to implement a training schedule to ensure that those who are learning the new model have opportunities to learn in manageable "chunks" and can implement and experiment before moving on to the next module. Generally speaking, plan on your training schedule to last at least one year for basic learning, then another year for deep understanding. Decide how you will introduce the model (likely at a back-to-school PL day) and how you plan to break the model into manageable sections that will be learned and implemented throughout the year. Learning new models and implementing them into practice with fidelity takes time, even with the most experienced and talented faculty. To help you consider how this might unfold in your school or district, we provide a sample implementation schedule that starts with an overview of the model and its components in Year 1, followed by increasing depth and breadth of strategies in Year 2 (see pp. 44–47).

Our assumption here is that most teachers already have sufficient knowledge of teaching strategies to begin using the model, albeit in simple ways in their classroom—essentially, "learning by doing." Over time, as they use and encounter challenges in applying the model, they'll engage in real-time learning to expand the repertoire of teaching strategies they use to apply the model. We also include in the sample plan an array of intersession supports (configuration maps, exemplars and models, practical tools, and feedback from peers and coaches) as well as goals for implementation. It's worth noting that goals tend to have more buy-in when they're *shared* goals, so we encourage you *not* to prescribe them at the outset (as we've done here for illustrative purposes), but rather, develop them with teachers by asking them to balance what's reasonable with student needs.

Notice, too, that we've framed professional learning in bite-sized segments to give teachers time to absorb new knowledge and skills, apply them in classrooms, receive feedback, and reflect on and refine their practices. If this seems like a lot, it is. But it's the only way to change habits and develop new ones. So, professional learning should unfold at a pace that supports deep learning and application.

You'll note that our sample plan for Year 2 reflects input on areas where teachers want to expand their repertoire of research-based strategies—namely, the learning phase during which students consolidate and reflect on their learning through teacher checks for understanding, deliberate practice, and feedback from teachers. You could do this in Year 1 as well, of course. Our point here is to consider engaging teachers in guiding their own learning to ensure it's meaningful and relevant to them. That is, you might decide to skip over other teaching and learning strategies (e.g., note taking or generating and testing hypotheses) not because they're unimportant, but because your teachers report that they already have a good handle on them and prefer to prioritize strategies with which they feel less familiar or adept.

With all of this in mind, Tool 5 on pp. 52–53 can help you segment professional learning into episodes that teachers can absorb, specifying learning objectives for each learning activity, identifying resources to support teacher learning, and developing shared goals for how the professional learning will benefit students and what everyone will do to support one another's success.

Special considerations for district-level implementation

If you are implementing an instructional model at a district level, here are some additional questions to consider before you get started:

- Are instructional challenges consistent across your district? Or do schools face different needs or challenges that may require different specificity or pace of professional learning?
- Can you present the instructional model to secondary and primary teachers in the same way? Or do you need to adapt the model and/or professional learning for these groups?
- Are your schools ready to embrace peer-to-peer coaching? Or do you need to spend time getting teachers comfortable with having other adults in their classrooms?
- Are your school leaders and school leadership teams ready to serve as instructional leaders? Or do you need to prepare them to observe and provide teachers with feedback and coaching?

Prior to launching your initiative at the district level, we encourage you to identify and bring together a district-level leadership team comprised of leaders from each school. During this session, you should agree upon the data you will gather, how it will be gathered, and the timeline for doing so. Once you have identified your primary instructional challenges and the model you will implement, this group can help you to create a districtwide training and implementation plan that spans the first year to ensure understanding and buy-in of your initiative. This group can also help you to develop agreed-upon progress indicators for the effort and serve as a critical friends group as challenges or questions arise. Lastly, because clear, ongoing communication is critical to the success of any effort, we recommend you create a district microsite (internal and/or external) related to the model and its rollout to address questions or concerns from staff, faculty, and other stakeholders.

Table 5. Year 1 Sample Implementation Plan

Month	Focus	Objectives
August	Overview of the model	▸ Teachers understand the model and how to use it to design lessons and units ▸ Teachers will work together to develop lessons and to practice inviting and delivering feedback
September	Phase 1: Engage interest	▸ Teachers learn strategies to *hook student interest* ▸ Teachers work together to design lessons with strategies to *hook interest* ▸ Teachers develop IC maps for engaging interest
October	Phase 2: Set goals for learning	▸ Teachers learn strategies for creating *success criteria* ▸ Teachers work together to identify *success criteria* for upcoming lessons ▸ Teachers develop IC maps for setting goals for learning
November	Phase 3: Guide new learning	▸ Teachers learn strategies to guide learning, especially *higher-order questions* ▸ Teachers plan lessons with *higher-order questions* together ▸ Teachers develop IC maps for ideal use of *questions*
January	Phase 4: Consolidate and reflect on learning	▸ Teachers learn strategies to consolidate learning, including *cooperative learning* ▸ Teachers select and plan to use *cooperative learning* protocols in lessons ▸ Teachers develop IC maps for ideal *cooperative learning*
March	Phase 5: Apply new learning	▸ Teachers learn strategies to apply learning, especially *independent practice* ▸ Teachers plan *independent practice* activities together ▸ Teachers develop IC maps for student performance
May	Reflect and celebrate	▸ Teachers share successes, including impact on learning ▸ Teachers identify ongoing challenges

Supports	Goals
▸ School leaders create opportunities for triads to engage in observation and peer coaching ▸ Teachers receive model lessons for all grade levels and subject areas	▸ All teachers use the model to design and deliver lessons ▸ Teachers share lessons ▸ All teachers participate in at least 3 classroom visits over a 6-week period
▸ Teachers receive packet of engagement activities ▸ Coaches observe and give feedback to triads on lesson "hooks" ▸ Peers observe and share feedback on "hooks"	▸ 75% of lessons reflect ideal use of *engagement strategies* ▸ Student surveys show increased engagement ▸ All teachers engage in three classroom observations
▸ Teachers receive success criteria exemplars ▸ Coaches give feedback to triads on *success criteria* ▸ Peers observe and share feedback on *success criteria*	▸ 80% of lessons reflect ideal use of *success criteria* ▸ Student surveys show increased clarity about goals ▸ All teachers engage in three classroom observations
▸ Teachers receive exemplars for questions ▸ Coaches give feedback to triads on classroom *questions* ▸ Peers observe and share feedback on *questions*	▸ 60% of lessons reflect ideal use of *questions* ▸ Student surveys show increased classroom participation ▸ All teachers engage in three classroom observations
▸ Teachers receive protocols for cooperative learning ▸ Coaches observe and give feedback to triads on *cooperative learning* ▸ Peers observe and share feedback on *cooperative learning*	▸ 75% of lessons reflect ideal use of *cooperative learning* protocols ▸ Formative assessment data show increased learning ▸ All teachers engage in three classroom observations
▸ Teachers receive protocols for cooperative learning ▸ Coaches give *independent practice* activities ▸ Peers review and provide feedback on student work	▸ All units engage students in *independent practice* ▸ Formative assessment data show increased learning ▸ Student surveys show increased confidence in learning
▸ Planning time for teams to refine lessons and units	▸ Start next year with well-developed unit plans

Table 6. Year 2 Sample Implementation Plan

Month	Focus	Objectives
August	Reflect on and go deeper in using the model	▸ Teachers share lessons that worked last year ▸ Teachers learn strategies for going deeper with the model ▸ Teachers collaboratively identify new learning needs
September	Dig deeper into Phase 2: Set goals for learning	▸ Teachers learn strategies to help *students set goals* and connect effort to success ▸ Teachers create lessons that connect effort with success ▸ Teachers develop IC maps for student goal setting
October	Dig deeper into Phase 3: Guide new learning	▸ Teachers learn strategies for using *nonlinguistic representations* to guide learning ▸ Teachers work together to incorporate *nonlinguistic representations* in lessons ▸ Teachers develop IC maps for use of *nonlinguistic representations*
November	Dig deeper into Phase 4: Consolidate and reflect on learning	▸ Teachers learn strategies for *checking for understanding* ▸ Teachers work together to build *checks for understanding* into lessons ▸ Teachers develop IC maps for *checks for understanding*
January	Dig deeper into Phase 4: Consolidate and reflect on learning	▸ Teachers learn strategies for *deliberate practice* ▸ Teachers design *deliberate practice* activities together ▸ Teachers *work with students* to develop IC maps for engaging in *deliberate practice*
March	Dig deeper into Phase 4: Consolidate and reflect on learning	▸ Teachers learn strategies for providing *motivating feedback* ▸ Teachers practice delivering written and oral *student feedback* ▸ Teachers develop IC maps for *teacher feedback*
May	Reflect and celebrate	▸ Teachers share successes, including impact on learning ▸ Teachers identify new professional learning needs

Supports	Goals
▸ Online tools for sharing lesson plans and engaging in virtual coaching ▸ Reading materials and guides for going deeper with the model	▸ All teachers contribute at least one exemplary lesson to the database ▸ Teachers continue to participate in three classroom visits over a 6-week period
▸ Teachers receive tools for student goal setting ▸ Coaches give triads feedback on student goal setting ▸ Peers observe and share feedback on student goal setting	▸ All students set unit learning and effort goals ▸ Student surveys show increased ownership of goals ▸ All teachers engage in three classroom observations and feedback sessions
▸ Teachers receive exemplary *nonlinguistic learning* activities ▸ Coaches give triads feedback on use of *nonlinguistic learning* ▸ Peers observe and share feedback on *nonlinguistic learning*	▸ All units include *nonlinguistic learning* activities ▸ Student surveys show increased grasp of concepts ▸ All teachers engage in three classroom observations and feedback sessions
▸ Teachers receive exemplary *checks for understanding* ▸ Coaches give triads feedback on *checks for understanding* ▸ Peers observe and share feedback on *checks for understanding*	▸ 80% of lessons include *checks for understanding* ▸ Student surveys show increased grasp of concepts ▸ All teachers engage in three classroom observations and feedback sessions
▸ Teachers receive exemplary *deliberate practice* assignments ▸ Coaches give triads feedback on *deliberate practice* activities ▸ Peers share and provide feedback on student artifacts from *deliberate practice*	▸ 80% of units include *deliberate practice* assignments ▸ Student surveys show increased self-talk during practice ▸ Teacher teams focus three feedback sessions on *deliberate practice*
▸ Teachers receive exemplary *motivating feedback* assignments ▸ Coaches give triads feedback on *student feedback* ▸ Peers review and provide feedback on one another's written *student feedback*	▸ Students receive *feedback* on all key assignments ▸ Student surveys show most find teacher feedback helpful ▸ Teacher teams focus three feedback sessions on *student feedback*
▸ Planning time for teams to refine lessons and units and codify exemplary units into database	▸ Start next year with 50% of lessons and units captured in database

Final reflection and checklist

Reflecting together

Here are some questions to reflect on as a school or district-level R&I Team:

1. What is our moral purpose for engaging in this effort? Do we have a common moral purpose, or several different underlying reasons for engaging in this work?

2. What can we do to generate staff buy-in, support—and even enthusiasm—for this effort?

3. What is our current level of urgency for implementing the model? Are we OK if it takes 2–3 years before it's fully and deeply implemented in every classroom? What time frame would be too short for us? Too long?

4. What do we feel is the right balance to strike between guiding teacher learning versus inviting them to identify their own learning needs?

5. Momentum for new initiatives often slows as the year progresses. What fun incentives or "self-care" activities could we provide during the "sagging middle" of the school year to help teachers stay focused and engaged?

6. Do we anticipate there may be staff who face difficulties in adopting the model (or leaders who may struggle to roll it out in their schools)? What emotional or professional support might they need? Who could mentor them?

Checklist for planning for success

- ☐ Develop and execute a plan to share the model with staff, including how it was selected/developed, using Tool 4.
- ☐ Select training option (external consultant, training-of-trainer, study groups), using Tool 4.
- ☐ Identify goals and measures of success for the overall effort, using Tool 5.
- ☐ Generate enthusiasm for the model in a launch event that connects it with moral purpose.
- ☐ Identify key components of the model and descriptors of ideal use in the classroom, using Tool 6.
- ☐ Create a plan for professional learning in short segments for learning and application.
- ☐ Identify tools and resources to support teacher implementation of the model in classrooms.
- ☐ Create (or utilize existing) structure for peer coaching teams, including feedback protocols, using Tools 7 and 8.
- ☐ Engage teachers in peer-to-peer classroom observations and feedback conversations.
- ☐ Take time to celebrate success and plan next steps in professional learning with teachers.

Check out
Chapter 4 Tools
on the following pages

Tool 4: Deciding on your approach to professional learning

Step 1: Consider your options

Option	Pros	Cons
Hire a consultant	Good way to kick off the school year, especially if adopting the model Deep knowledge of content Seasoned facilitator Can deliver ongoing support	Expensive Will need to rely on for refresher training or training for new hires May insist on fidelity to their model, making this a less viable option for adapting a model
Train-the-trainer	Develop in-house capacity and sustainability Allows your team to *adapt* a particular model with terminology that fits your culture Teachers may respond better to "one of their own" sharing new ideas with them	Expensive Relies on the team's skills for learning and teaching the process Relies on informal, but well-respected leaders
Collaborative inquiry	Most cost effective Ideal if you have developed your own model	Lacks insights and motivational qualities of outside expert or trained internal team Requires a well-established collegial learning community
Focus on "early adopters"	Create a coalition of the willing Apt to move forward more quickly Teach through example Can work out any kinks or issues with the model early on	Lacks focused, schoolwide initiative Early use of the model may be slow, sporadic, and inconsistent Lacks formal training

Step 2: Rank your criteria

First, go down the first blank column and assign a weighting to cost, fidelity of training, and adaptation needs of the training option. (How important is the cost of training to me? How important is it to me that the training sticks to the intended model? How important is adapting the model to our culture?)

Then fill in the second column for each model being considered. (Is this expensive? Would the training model have fidelity to the intended model? Could we adapt this to our culture through this training method?)

Then, multiply your weighting by the score. For example, if your team ranked the cost as very important (4) and the training option as very expensive (1), that training method would only get a score of 4. On the other hand, if the cost isn't as important (2) and the training is cheap (4), that method would get a score of 8.

	Importance of this criterion (1=low; 4=high)	How the option ranks	Final weighted score
Cost (expense) (1=high; 4=low)			
Fidelity of training (1=low; 4=high)			
Need for adaptation to your culture (1=low; 4=high)			

Tool 5: Professional learning planning worksheet

Time	Over what time period will we embed new knowledge and skills in classroom practice?
Focus	What new knowledge and skills will we develop?
Objectives	What will teachers know and be able to do by the end of the 6–8-week period? What learning tasks will they engage in during the professional learning sessions? What artifacts will emerge from the professional learning sessions?

Supports	What resources will teachers receive to support their learning and use of new strategies in the classroom?
	Where will teacher coaches focus their guidance for teacher teams?
	Where will peer coaches focus their observations and feedback?
Goals	What differences will we see in classrooms over the next 6–8 weeks from what we learn?
	What differences will we see for students in the next 6–8 weeks from what we learn?
	What will we do together to accomplish our goals?

Tool 6: Creating an innovation configuration map

Creating an innovation configuration (IC) map is an effective way to help teachers gain clarity about expectations and move them toward more effective use of better practices. An IC map identifies the major components of a program, practice, or change initiative (i.e., an innovation) and describes how each element looks along a continuum from weak or low-level implementation to ideal or high-fidelity implementation (Hall & Hord, 2015).

Creating IC maps in "bottom-up" fashion—that is, in collaboration with teachers—not only supports shared understanding of behaviors and expectations related to implementation, but also encourages teacher and leader reflection, feedback, and requests for assistance during an implementation effort (Hord, Stiegelbauer, Hall, & George, 2006)—often with little or no top-down intervention or compulsion.

Here's how it works. Once you have your objectives outlined, have your teachers break into grade-alike teams to discuss what they hope to see for each of these objectives. Following are a few examples to get you started. For each objective, (a) represents the ideal while (c) represents bare minimum or unacceptable.

Objective: Engage students in understanding and personalizing the overall objective of the lesson.

(a) IDEAL	(b) ADEQUATE	(c) UNACCEPTABLE
Students actively discuss what they are going to learn, what they already know, and what they might be able to do as a result of this lesson.	Teacher outlines the lesson's objectives and pauses for questions before moving on to the lesson.	Teacher dives right into the lesson without including the objective or outcomes.

Tool 7: Inviting feedback protocol

Use this feedback protocol to help your peer observations be informative, nonthreatening, and provide a platform for 2-way conversations.

Observer name: _____

Name of teacher inviting the peer observation: _____

Time/date of lesson and duration: _____

Lesson topic: _____

Look-fors	Observation Notes/Questions	Teacher self-reflection (to be completed after the observation and discussion)
When you observe my lesson, here are 2–3 things I'd really like you to focus on: _____ _____ _____		
One instructional challenge I'm currently working on: _____ _____		
One classroom management challenge I'm currently working on: _____ _____		
One highlight I'm really proud of: _____ _____		

Tool 8: Peer coaching conversation protocol

Sentence stem	Purpose of the question	Notes
The bright spots I saw in your lesson today were:	To celebrate the successes that can be replicated.	Consider 2–3, not just one.
Tell me more about why you chose to . . .	To encourage teacher meta-cognition.	Empathize with the teacher's thinking. Even if things didn't go as well as planned, acknowledge that all teachers experience best-laid plans going awry or not taking advantage of a learning opportunity when it arose.
Here were some missed opportunities I saw:	To guide the teacher toward reconsidering actions when a student is experiencing difficulty.	Keep these to 1–2.
I wonder . . . or How might you… or Have you considered . . .	To offer ideas in a nonthreatening way while also encouraging the teacher to offer ideas.	As many of these ideas as possible should come from the teacher. Offer a method that has worked for you, then let him/her brainstorm aloud.
I'm going to forward a few resources that you might find helpful.	To encourage self-reflection and growth after the conversation ends.	Offer 1–2, but don't overwhelm your colleague with a laundry list of books and websites.

Example:

After observing the geometry lesson, the observer met with the teacher to debrief.

She started with the positive: "I saw so many bright spots in this unit! Your students were engaged right away with the pool table and started having some early guesses on the ball's trajectory that were right-on. I'm not sure they would have grasped this or gravitated to the topic as quickly with a more traditional approach."

Then she started the reflection: "Tell me more about what you observed when students had to go from the golf ball activity to understanding the relationship between degrees and angles."

The teacher agreed that there was a gap in the process and that not all students were able to make that leap easily. They talked about a missed opportunity: one additional lesson that would simply have had students understand the concept of 360° and its importance in our daily lives. This would have led to a more natural progression to the angles activity.

While brainstorming activities, they discuss a homework assignment where students take home a cardstock template of a circular protractor with the assignment to find things in their homes that are 45, 90, 180, and 270 degrees. The observer ends by sending along a PDF of the template and a short animated movie about measuring angles for the students to watch.

The overall discussion is that of two professionals reflecting, brainstorming, and creating ideas together. At no time did the teacher feel judged or inadequate. As a matter of fact, her observer borrowed many of the ball activities for her own lessons the following week.

Chapter 5: Managing and overcoming resistance to change

Julia sits at her kitchen table on a sunny late-winter Saturday morning. Normally, she would be at the park for a run. Instead she finds herself musing over two teachers giving her and her leadership team the most grief with the "new" instructional model. It's not really even "new" anymore, she thinks ruefully. We've been at this for seven months now. At her R&I Team meeting the day before, several of her coaches wondered aloud what to do with the two teachers who weren't getting on board with the new model. She knows that one, Danielle, is a new teacher who's already struggling with classroom management issues. Dropping an instructional model into the mix appears to have put her over the edge. She seems constantly overwhelmed, near tears, and at times even resentful and angry. "I've got four I.E.P.s to work on already and can barely keep up with lesson plans and now they're asking me to do this?" she reportedly groused in the faculty lounge.

With her dog pawing at the kitchen door to go outside, Julia grabs its leash and decides to take a walk. Once outside, she breathes in some fresh air and begins to feel a bit more tranquil and generous toward Danielle and AJ, both of whom have great promise as educators. She puts herself in their shoes. Perhaps Danielle's assigned mentor—a no-nonsense veteran who can sometimes give the appearance of talking down to people—is complicating matters by making Danielle feel even more flustered. Perhaps she'd feel less overwhelmed if she could interact with peers a little closer to her age, who remember what it feels like to be an overwrought first-year teacher. Two people, one of whom is already on the R&I Team, immediately come to mind who can show Danielle how to manage her classroom and lend a helping hand with lesson planning (if not lend her some lessons to use). Julia makes a mental note to reach out to them on Monday.

For AJ, a mid-career changer who likely didn't get much pedagogical preparation in his alternate route to the classroom, the model may be revealing some inadequacies he feels as a teacher but doesn't want to admit as he's been in the classroom for so long. Julia and AJ are nearly the same age and share a camaraderie as "veterans" of the school—with AJ providing an irreverent yin to Julia's buttoned-up yang, something they've joked about. She knows AJ sees himself as free-spirited and spontaneous, so following a model of instruction rubs him the wrong way. He's made comments, in fact, about the need to seize upon "teachable moments" and "go with the flow" of learning.

"That's it!" she says aloud, startling her dog. *The flow of learning.* At its heart, that's what the instructional model is all about—developing shared understanding of the *flow of learning* and mapping instructional strategies onto it. AJ is a semi-professional musician—and a pretty good one at that, playing gigs at a local coffee shop and other places around town. Earlier that year, in fact, he'd sponsored a lunchtime student singer-songwriter club and subsequent talent show. *Only PG lyrics,* she'd reminded him with a smile and been amazed at the quality of songs students had written and performed while following a *model* AJ had given them: *Verse-chorus-verse-chorus-bridge-verse-chorus-chorus.* Instructional design was no different—and no less a constraint on teacher creativity than song structure was for songwriters.

She decides to invite AJ out for coffee the next week to share her insights with him over an informal chat as peers, rather than in a formal meeting "in the principal's office." During their chat, she'll help him to see how the instructional model doesn't conflict with his ideals and beliefs as an educator at all; he can still be creative while following the model. Moreover, it will help him to become *even better* at what he does—just like the song structure he'd shown students to make their songs better. ~

Brace yourself: Resistance to change is gonna come

What Julia experienced in this anecdote is what any leader who engages in a change effort worth undertaking undoubtedly faces at some point: resistance to change. With any initiative, some people will embrace the change enthusiastically and others will resist. This is certainly true of a change so central to a school's functioning as the introduction of an instructional model. Some teachers may be overjoyed that the needs and challenges they've long wrung their hands about are finally being addressed by the model. Others may dispute that there was ever a problem in the first place or quibble with the solution (in this case, the model you've chosen). For example,

- You may find some faculty struggling to apply the model in their classroom and complaining that it's unworkable or impractical.

- Some dissident voices may object to the model on more intellectual grounds, calling out flaws in the chosen model and/or attempting to discredit the research.

- Others may be scandalized at the prospect of peers observing their lessons or accuse you of undermining their professional autonomy.

- Others may sniff that your chosen model is "only for the bad kids" or is an affront to their deeply held beliefs about the "right way" to teach kids.

As we'll see, these objections reflect common themes in why people resist change, which are often rooted in the underlying ways people absorb new ideas—that is, their thinking preferences. At times, people may voice their misgivings about change in outright resistance, folding their arms figuratively (or literally) in defiance. Others may nod along and seem to support the effort, yet be thinking all the while, "This, too, shall pass," and thus, do little to actually change their classroom practices. Either way, whether the resistance is overt or more subtle (read: passive-aggressive) the result is the same: Your change effort will reflect what education historian Larry Cuban (1984) has observed about education initiatives often being like a storm at sea: "The surface is agitated and turbulent, while the ocean floor is calm and serene (if a bit murky)" (p. 234).

Here's the bottom line: If you haven't already heard such objections, you soon will. And if you *never hear any* grumblings or misgivings about adopting a new instructional model in classrooms, take heed: People may simply be passive-aggressively not implementing the model or hoping a crisis will come along that will cause you and the other members of the R&I Team to lose interest and move onto something else. Basically, if people *are* grumbling, uncomfortable, or unhappy, that's OK; it means you've moved them out of their comfort zones to a point that we'll soon see is called "conscious incompetence"—when people realize they lack the skills or knowledge to do something well. That's an important (and unavoidable) part of any change. In fact, it's difficult, if not impossible, to get better at something if we don't first realize we don't know how to do it—or must get better at doing it.

Of course, you don't want people in your school or district to *keep* grumbling forever. That's not good for anyone. So, this chapter will give you insights into what's actually behind people's objections when they resist change (and the predictable patterns they reflect) and what you can do to not just *overcome* people's objections, but actually help them to *embrace* and advocate for change. As the old saying goes, there's no zealot like a convert. So, our hope is that by reading and implementing the insights from this chapter, you'll be able to get your entire school (or district) zealously committed to change.

This is your brain on change

To understand why people resist change, let's explore some research, starting with an intriguing theory advanced by several researchers and writers—including the work of Carl Jung, Anthony F. Gregorc, Ned Herrmann, Katharine Cook Briggs and Isabel Briggs Myers, and Donald O. Clifton of the Gallup Organization—that essentially states that people respond differently to challenges based upon their dominant *thinking preferences*. Loosely speaking, these frameworks reflect dichotomies in how different people *perceive* information (e.g., concrete/verbal/rational analysis vs. holistic/intuitive/visual intuition) and how they *process* information (application-oriented/impulsive *doing* vs. meaning-making/contemplative *reflecting*). These thinking preferences appear to reflect different kinds of thinking thought to occur in what's been called *left-brain* versus *right-brain* thinking (Herrmann, 1998) and what Daniel Kahneman (2011) has referred to as *fast* versus *slow* thinking, which, respectively, help us to automate complex tasks (e.g., reading, riding a bike, and picking up on others' nonverbal cues) versus engaging in effortful thinking (e.g., pondering a new idea or dissecting a logical argument). So, when you put *left-right* plus *fast-slow* together, you get these four thinking preferences:

1. **Analytical, logical *thinkers***. Our *left* brains are home to logical analysis. Thus *slow, left-brain* thinking is thought to be objective and analytical. People who demonstrate this thinking preference are often regarded as clear-headed and objective. Like Sergeant Friday of the old *Dragnet* TV series, they insist on "just the facts" before being ready to move forward with a change initiative. People who default to this mode of *slow* thinking tend to be cautious, objective, and analytical—sometimes overly so causing them to suffer from paralysis by analysis. They may also take seeming delight in poking holes in others' plans and resisting change if they're not certain it's the absolute right (or most logical) course to take.

2. **Sequential, action-oriented *doers*.** Automation of *left-brain* functioning reflects sequence and routine. People with this thinking preference are said to be pragmatic and action-focused ("get 'er done" types, to use the Southern colloquialism), though others may view them as hasty, judgmental, or overly compliance-oriented. While they can be the first to act when the way forward is clear (apt to say, "Just tell me what to do and I'll do it"), they may be reluctant to move forward until all of the details are sorted out or they're being asked to relearn something that's become a comfortable routine for them.

3. **Imaginative, big-picture *energizers*.** Our so-called *right* brains are home to gestalt and big-picture synthesis. Thus, people who default to *right-brain*, *slow* thinking are imaginative, like playing with "big ideas," and are comfortable with changing their own mental paradigms—as well as getting others to see and buy into their vision. At times, though, they can drive others to distraction by skipping over details or bouncing from one idea to the next. And they may drag their heels if they can't see or buy into the larger vision of where things are going.

4. **Interpersonal, social-oriented *connectors*.** Our *right* brains are also considered the source of empathy—the result of *fast* thinking that quickly sizes up others' facial and nonverbal cues. People with this thinking preference concern themselves with (and tend to readily detect) undercurrents in group dynamics, and are often adept with building esprit de corps. At times, though, their "I'm OK, you're OK" tendencies and desire to preserve group cohesion may come across as unwillingness to rock the boat when change in the status quo is needed. 1.2.3.4.

In the following table, we summarize how these various thinking preferences appear in several common personality/thinking preference frameworks.

Table 7: Popular thinking preference frameworks

Framework	Left-slow	Left-fast	Right-slow	Right-fast
Herrmann	Analytical	Practical	Experimental	Relational
DiSC	Conscientiousness	Dominance	Influence	Steadiness
CliftonStrengths	Strategic thinking	Executing	Influencing	Relationship
Emergenetics	Analytical	Structural	Conceptual	Social

It's worth noting that these ideas of left and right brain, and slow versus fast thinking, are more metaphor than neuroscience, as brain researchers haven't actually found that brain activity occurs neatly in one side of the brain or another or been able to isolate a slow or fast-thinking part of the brain (Hines, 1987; Kahneman, 2011). Moreover, although these models of learning styles have been around for decades, little hard scientific evidence has yet to emerge to definitively prove their existence (Coffield, Moseley, Hall, & Ecclestone, 2004). That said, a new generation of neuroscience studies are appearing to validate some of the core underpinnings of cognitive styles. They've found, for example, that people who report a preference for visual versus verbal learning also showed different brain activity patterns and eye movements when engaged in solving the same task (Bendall, Galpin, Marrow, & Cassidy, 2016). They may thus be confirming what people as far back as the ancient Greeks and Egyptians observed: namely, that human beings have distinct personality types or ways of thinking and interacting with the world. Engineers, for instance, usually aren't great poets, and actuarial scientists typically don't make for good grief counselors—and vice versa.

Sailing into stormy seas

So, what does any of this have to do with bringing an instructional model to your school or district? Perhaps quite a lot. Years ago, a team of researchers at McREL conducted a large meta-analysis of research on school leadership (Marzano, Waters, & McNulty, 2005). By far, the big take-away was that better school leadership was linked to better student achievement and that strong leadership was comprised of 21 key responsibilities. However, one perplexing finding also emerged. As we described in *Balanced Leadership for Powerful Learning* (Goodwin, Cameron, & Hein, 2015), a few outlier studies among the dozens of studies in the meta-analysis actually found *negative* correlations between better leadership behaviors and student achievement. In other words, in some schools, principals who seemed to demonstrate all the right leadership behaviors had *lower* levels of achievement in their schools. The researchers wondered if one explanation for this paradox might be that the same leader who provides a steady hand on the tiller in smooth waters (and thus, be regarded as a good leader), may struggle to guide his or her team through stormy seas or times of dramatic change. To get to the bottom of this question, the research team synthesized several studies on change and found that when the going gets tough, people often resist change for one of four reasons:

1. They view the change as an unnecessary **break from the past**—they don't comprehend the **logic** for it or remain unconvinced of its necessity.

2. They **lack the skills or knowledge** they need to carry out the change—they are unclear exactly what to do or need more **details** before they're ready to move forward.

3. They feel the change conflicts with their **ideals and beliefs**—they don't understand or share the **big picture** vision or moral purpose for the change.

4. They sense the change conflicts with **group norms**—they feel the change is disrupting social harmony or upending their own social status.

In a follow-up survey of 900 principals, the researchers sought to tease out (among other things) whether the kinds of change schools were experiencing (relatively routine "first order," incremental, smooth sailing-type improvements versus more complex "second-order," stormy seas-type changes) had any bearing on how people perceived the effectiveness of their leaders.

To a large degree, that's exactly what they found. In particular, they discovered that *four* leadership responsibilities were *negatively* correlated with second-order change—that is, in schools buffeted by complex changes, leaders were seen as falling short in these areas:

1. **Input**—people felt excluded from important decisions about the change effort
2. **Order**—people felt the school lacked standard operating procedures or routines
3. **Communication**—people required greater clarity and more dialogue with leaders
4. **Culture**—people felt a diminished sense of group cohesion and personal well-being

Connecting the dots

Consider those previous lists: *four* thinking preferences, *four* ways people resist change, and *four* leadership behaviors that suffer when people resist change. We might connect these dots this way:

1. If **analytical, logical *thinkers*** feel change is an *illogical break from the past*, they may require opportunities for **input** so they can participate in the logic of decision making.
2. If **sequential, action-oriented *doers*** *lack the skills or knowledge* to do what's being asked of them, they may feel the need to quickly re-establish routines and **order**.
3. If **imaginative, big-picture *energizers*** believe change *conflicts with their ideals*, they're apt to crave two-way **communication** with leaders to ensure they share the same vision.
4. If **interpersonal, social-oriented *connectors*** feel change *conflicts with group norms*, they sense something amiss with the **culture** and seek to restore well-being and cohesion.

We'll bet that reading this list provided you with some "aha" moments and new insights into particular people on your team, in your school, or even in your family. That said, you should avoid pigeonholing people into one or another particular group, as researchers have found that people don't always fit neatly into a single category; most of us engage, at some point, in all four types of thinking. This flexibility is, in fact, a bone of contention for critics of thinking preferences, who argue if people don't fall into consistent categories, the whole theory must be bunk (Willingham, Hughes, & Dobolyi, 2015). The reality, though, is probably that we ought to consider thinking preferences as akin to "hats" we all wear, even though we may prefer one or two more than others.

Leaders must be out of their minds

Here, we might safely draw this point: Managing change is not a one-size-fits-all proposition. Just as teachers need to differentiate instruction, so too, leaders must differentiate leadership for those they're leading. That requires getting out of your own head or switching "hats" long enough to appreciate that others may not respond to change (or want to be led) the same way as you.

Consider, for example, that as leaders:

- **Analytical thinkers** may assume people will be wowed by charts and graphs demonstrating the inescapable logic of their position, yet followers may be uninspired or disconnected from their vision. Or such leaders may assume others appreciate their thoughtful conscientiousness as they mentally play out every angle; meanwhile, their followers may simply want them to try something, *anything*, to see if it works.

- **Big-picture energizers** may assume they can captivate people with their vision and let the details sort themselves out, assuming that, like them, people prefer to learn by doing and resent overly detailed guidance; meanwhile, their followers may need specifics and opportunities to wrap their heads around the logic of the change before they're ready to move ahead.

- **Action-oriented doers** might assume others appreciate their decisiveness and clarity and will fall in line with clear, explicit goals and a to-do list of next steps, yet followers may question their logic, wonder where they're going, or be looking around the room to see if anyone's upset by the hasty action.

- **Interpersonal connectors** may assume others appreciate their efforts to create group cohesion and camaraderie through ongoing collaboration and shared decision making, yet followers may fear they're on a complacent sinking ship that needs some shaking up and someone to tell them they're wrong.

In the end, perhaps the biggest thing leaders can take from all of this is that when leading change, they ought to address the whole mind, which, as it turns out, maps nicely onto what leadership theorist William Bridges (1991) long ago described as the 4 P's for managing change. In short, when experiencing change, people feel a loss of control, which leaders can restore by

- giving people *input* to logically understand the **Purpose** of the effort,
- restoring a sense of *order* by describing clear next steps, or a **Plan,** for getting there,
- creating opportunities for *communication* and dialogue to see the big **Picture,** and
- attending to a disrupted *culture* and restoring well-being by showing everyone their **Part**.

So, now that we've explored the deeply personal, emotional, and intellectual reasons people resist change, let's see what it's likely to look like in your school or district as you attempt to roll out your instructional model, starting with a phenomenon that's probably too familiar to every school leader: a proliferation of "yabbits."

The secret life of yabbits

You likely know what we're talking about here. No doubt you've seen it happen: Someone presents a new idea at a staff meeting. After a pause comes the reply, "Yeah . . . but [fill in the blank]." Often, what comes next may be a legitimate concern—and one that likely reflects, in some way, one of the four reasons we know people resist change. The trouble with these "Yeah . . . buts" (*yabbits*) is that if they're left unanswered, like real rabbits, they begin to multiply. Soon, you've got yabbits hopping all around your school, leaving little droppings of negativity everywhere—in the faculty lounge, in the parking lot, in team meetings.

When it comes to adopting an instructional model, we might imagine yabbits saying things like the following:

- "Yabbit there's no *one way* to teach all kids. You have to differentiate."
- "Yabbit what I'm doing works. Why should I have to redo all my lessons?"
- "Yabbit this will suck the joy and spontaneity out of teaching."
- "Yabbit this undermines our professional wisdom and autonomy."

Consider for a moment where each of these yabbits may be coming from—that is, what *thinking preference* or common reason for resisting change may underlie their misgivings. As you'll see in a moment, understanding why people resist change—and the underlying reasons for their resistance—can help you address their concerns in real time, and even better, anticipate them beforehand.

Now, let's imagine for a moment that, understanding why people resist change, we could superimpose subtitles on each of these yabbits. We might see something like this:

- "Yabbit there's no *one way* to teach all kids. You have to differentiate." [Subtitle: *I'm upset no one asked for my input and/or I don't see the logic or rationale for this.*]
- "Yabbit what I'm doing works. Why should I have to redo all my lessons?" [Subtitle: *I don't like being moved out of my comfort zone or feeling incompetent.*]
- "Yabbit this will suck the joy and spontaneity out of teaching." [Subtitle: *I don't see the big picture and/or I'm afraid what we're doing here may conflict with my beliefs.*]
- "Yabbit this undermines our professional wisdom and autonomy." [Subtitle: *I value my social status and don't want to look bad in front of my peers and/or I think others may be upset.*]

Putting the yabbits to rest

So, now that you know what's behind people's objections, it's a little easier to see how to address them. Here, we return to McREL's research on leadership and, in particular, the four areas where people's perception of leadership is known to suffer when they're experiencing complex, second-order change (which we sometimes refer to as the "unholy four"):

- Perceived lack of input on the decision-making process.
- Perceived lack of communication about the new changes or the plan.
- Perceived sense that the school is abandoning its time-honored culture.
- Perceived sense that leaders are failing to provide order and routines.

In the following table, we identify the four areas of resistance and what you can do as an R&I Team to overcome resistance in each area.

Table 8: Understanding and overcoming resistance to change

Concerns (you hear phrases like . . .)	Underlying issue	Leadership response
"I don't know why we're doing this." "What problem are we trying to solve?" "Why did we choose this model?" "Are we sure it's the right one?"	People tend to resist change when they don't understand the **logic** or rationale for the change. As a result, the change feels like an unwarranted—if not illogical—**break from the past**. In short, people want to know a) what's the problem and b) how do we know this is the right solution?	These stakeholders are apt to complain of lack of **input** on the logic of your decision-making. So, start by helping others see how the lack of an instructional model is a problem by sharing data, observations, and research, and then soliciting their input as you select the model. In short, engage others to help them understand the **purpose** of what you're doing.
"This will suck the spontaneity and joy out of learning." "It's too sage-on-the-stage." "It's prescriptive and mechanical." "What about teacher creativity and teachable moments?"	People tend to resist change if they feel conflicts with deeply held **ideals and beliefs**. Some may voice a vague gut feeling that something is "off" about the change. Others may be explicit, even calling into question your moral purpose and whether you share their concern for students.	These stakeholders are apt to complain about lack of **communication** even when you feel you've been clear and even repetitious with messaging. Often, what's really happening is people need *dialogue* to feel heard as well as hear your ideals and beliefs and how the change aligns with them. In short, through two-way dialogue, create a positive **picture** of where you're going.
"Everybody feels second-guessed and professionally demeaned." "All this teamwork is inefficient." "These observations are disrupting my class." "Honestly, I don't have much to learn from my peers."	People tend to resist change that disrupts **group norms**—which are often *implicit*, including teacher autonomy, not sharing lesson plans, or working only with a preferred group of colleagues. Thus, a seemingly simple change like peer coaching can be incredibly disruptive and, if not framed carefully, sow distrust.	These stakeholders are apt to complain about the new **culture** (and/or vanishing old culture) in the school. Thus, you may need to make explicit your *new norms*, including that teachers will work together, share lessons, and observe each other in order to *enhance* (not *erode*) professionalism via collegial sharing and dialogue. In doing so, you'll show everyone their **part** in the change.
"This new model is no better than what I was doing before." "I still don't know what I'm supposed to be doing." "We haven't gotten enough PL." "There's no way you can expect me to do all of this well right now."	People tend to resist change if they feel they **lack the skills or knowledge** to successfully carry out the change. They may complain that their old way of teaching was better, they don't have enough clarity about what's expected, need more PL, or that expectations for "ideal use" of the model are unrealistic.	These stakeholders are apt to complain that leaders are failing to provide a proper sense of **order** or routines in the school, or that new routines (e.g., lesson plan templates) are unworkable. Here, you'll need to help others adopt new routines with clear examples of what's expected as well as plenty of opportunities for learning and developing new skills.

As noted earlier, people's thinking preferences are often behind the reasons they resist change. That said, such categories aren't always hard-and-fast; with any given change, any individual might resist for a variety of reasons (though they may be more apt to resist for reasons that relate to their strongest thinking preference or two). So, the point here isn't that you need to tailor responses to individuals, but rather, ensure that you're anticipating any number of reasons people may resist change and addressing them beforehand. Basically, by identifying these root causes of change resistance (which may differ from faculty member to faculty member) you can take steps to mitigate the damage that change resistance might cause your efforts.

It's also important that you listen to and fully consider stakeholder concerns about change, and not simply dismiss them as yabbits, because they may be surfacing issues that reflect others' concerns or misgivings. For example, if you are moving too quickly through an implementation, and your faculty are trying to tell you just that, simply bulldozing through will not ultimately help your cause. Thus, you should pay close attention to how people are responding to change so you can determine whether the complaints stem from resistance to change or if, indeed, you need to rethink how you're managing your instructional model strategy.

Use Tool 9 on pp. 70–71 and Tool 10 on p. 72 to help you plan for, and respond to, resistance to change.

Leader, know thyself

As you've considered other people's thinking preferences, you've likely become more aware of your own as well. As we've noted earlier, it's important that you don't assume others share the same thinking preferences as you—or want to be led the same way you might want to be led.

- You may be a **big-picture visionary** who inspires others with bold, compelling ideas. You also respond well to simply being given the "big idea" for a change and sorting out the details as you go. But don't assume that everyone else is ready to move forward simply on the basis of seeing the vision and how great everything will be. Also, recognize that you're apt to grow frustrated when others don't share your vision. You may find yourself grumbling things like, "Well, I guess I'm the only one who cares enough about the kids to want to break the mold." If you find yourself saying something like this, take a moment to ask yourself if you've done enough to help others also understand the logic and purpose for you're doing, and their role in the change.

- You may be an **interpersonal connector**, using your social skills to build strong, cohesive teams, keep everyone engaged, and feel like part of the group. For you, as long as you know others are on board and how you'll work together, you're ready to press on. Don't assume, though, that simply creating positive peer pressure on your team will carry the day. If you start grousing, "These people are simply not team players; they're out of step with our culture and shared values," perhaps you should consider that you haven't done enough to paint a picture of where you're going, provide a plan for getting there, or engage people in the logic of your decision making.

- You may be an **analytical learner** who provides strong intellectual leadership, often seeing things that others don't, and you parse through data and glean insights from research and from others in your school. For you, as long as you're clear about the rationale for a change and convinced that others have done their homework, you're probably ready to move forward. Don't assume, though, that simply because you've connected dots for people and shown them the logic of your decision, that they're ready to move ahead. If you find yourself grumbling things like, "These people just don't want to face the facts. It's so obvious we've got to do this," you may need to spend some more time painting a positive picture of where you're going, providing details about how to get there, and addressing people's need to understand the role they'll play in the change.

- You may be a no-nonsense, **action-oriented commander** who often leads with confidence of conviction and leaves little doubt who needs to do what by when. You enjoy executing on a plan, so for you, receiving clear marching orders is often enough: Tell you what to do and you'll do it. Don't assume that's true of others or that they're being insubordinate when they seem to drag their heels, however. If you find yourself thinking or saying things like, "I'm sick of all the second-guessing and drama; we need less talk and more action," you may need to pause a moment to consider if people understand your logic and see as clearly as you do what will get better. Realize that you may be upending some norms and values, whether implicit or explicit.

The key takeaway here is that while people are often well suited to one, two, or even three of these roles, few leaders find that all four roles come naturally to them. Thus, you may need to "lean in" to the roles that come less naturally to you (even those that you may regard as less important). You almost certainly have people in your school who reflect all four categories of "yabbits." Ignore them at your peril. This is, in fact, what we mean by "balanced leadership" in our other publications—balancing these four roles to create successful school change and improvement.

Lastly, take a good look around your R&I Team. Quite likely, across the group, you can fill all four leadership roles quite nicely. So, in addition to sharing particular leadership tasks, you might also share specific leadership roles—ensuring that you're providing and sharing a vision, monitoring and executing on a plan, ensuring staff know their roles and feel engaged in the change, and involving them in shared decision making and learning.

Overcoming the implementation dip

Lastly, we want to warn you of something that's likely to happen as you set about implementing an instructional model in your school or district. It's an idea that comes from Michael Fullan, who in his work *Leading in a Culture of Change* (2001) coined the term "implementation dip"—the tendency for performance to slump after initiating a change, often when the fear of change collides with a lack of know-how. You're likely to see something similar as you encourage widespread adoption of an instructional model in your school or district for a variety of reasons, including these:

- **Initial incompetence.** At first, teachers' implementation of the model is apt to be clumsy or mechanical. In short, they may be doing the right things, but poorly, and thus the expected gains in student engagement and learning may be slow to come.
- **Push-back.** As we've noted throughout this chapter, it's common for people to resist change, especially if their initial efforts fall flat or "blow up" on them—something that's apt to happen anytime we try something new in the classroom.

- **Backsliding.** It's also common for teachers to slide back to old practices, something Mary Budd Rowe (1986) discovered years ago when she encouraged teachers to adopt the simple practice of using "wait time" when asking questions in class. After three or four weeks of embedding the new practice in their classrooms, many soon reverted to old habits.
- **Waning enthusiasm**. Often, following the initial excitement of a new initiative, a lull can follow during the "sagging middle" of the school year when fatigue sets in and sticking with the new practices begins to feel more laborious.
- **Unforeseen distractions**. Schools and districts are dynamic places, of course, where unforeseen events, new external directives, and other distractions can undo even the best laid plans.

To overcome implementation dips, Fullan encourages school leadership teams to:

- Maintain focus and urgency to quash any this-too-shall-pass syndrome
- Monitor implementation to avoid backsliding into familiar (yet inferior) practices
- Listen to naysayers and, as appropriate, incorporate their ideas into change efforts
- Work as teams to buck each other up when the going gets tough

By employing these strategies, you and your R&I Team should be able to overcome implementation dips and see real gains. As your data start trending upward, people will start pulling together, and things will feel different. You may feel a new culture of collaboration and collegiality take root, along with a general sense of optimism. Yet, none of that is possible without data to monitor, report, and celebrate. So, in the next chapter, we'll help you consider which data to track, how to set benchmark indicators and other goals, and perhaps, most importantly, how to ensure your school culture approaches data openly and with an eye toward improvement.

Final reflection and checklist

Here are some questions to reflect on as a school or district-level R&I Team and a checklist for guiding implementation of an instructional model.

Reflecting together

- Which teachers have embraced the model most enthusiastically? What did we do to help them to embrace the change?
- Which teachers are slow to adopt the model? What seem to be the underlying reasons? Can we categorize their resistance according to the four types identified in this chapter?
- Knowing why they may be resisting change, what else can we do to help them become more comfortable with the change?
- What leadership roles are each of us most comfortable playing? How might we balance one another?
- Have we painted a clear picture of where we're going? (For some inspiration, you may want to watch Patti Dobrowolski's TEDxRainier video "Draw Your Future.")

Checklist for managing and overcoming resistance to change

☐ Develop a change management plan (see Tools 9 and 10) to anticipate and overcome resistance to change.

☐ Articulate a vision or picture for the change.

☐ Articulate a rationale or purpose for the change.

☐ Articulate new norms—and if necessary, call out old, counterproductive norms—to help everyone understand their part in moving forward.

☐ Share your plan for moving forward (from the previous chapter).

*Check out **Chapter 5 Tools** on the following pages*

Tool 9: Responding to concerns or resistance

This tool will help you address stakeholder resistance to change.

Key concerns	Perceived gap	Prevalence?
▸ Concerns about decision process ▸ Questions if a problem exists ▸ Questioning identified solution	Lack of **input**	☐ Isolated ☐ Mixed ☐ Widespread
▸ Concerns about not feeling heard ▸ Questioning the overall direction ▸ Questioning if it's "right for kids"	Poor **communication**	☐ Isolated ☐ Mixed ☐ Widespread
▸ Concerns we're changing who we are as a school ▸ Feeling professionally disrespected	Declining **culture**	☐ Isolated ☐ Mixed ☐ Widespread
▸ Concerns about lack of skills or knowledge to implement model well ▸ Calls for more training	Declining sense of **order**	☐ Isolated ☐ Mixed ☐ Widespread

Who will help?	Action steps	Results

Tool 10: Planning to overcome resistance to change

Reasons for potential resistance	Potential response(s)	Your next steps
Failing to see the logic *Stakeholders view the instructional model as an unnecessary break from past practice, don't comprehend the logic for it, or remain unconvinced of its necessity.*	Solicit input when selecting model. Share selection criteria. Share research for models under consideration. Engage in book study or other forms of intellectual inquiry.	
Lacking skills or knowledge *Stakeholders lack the skills or knowledge they need to implement the model, are unclear what's expected, or need more details before they can move forward.*	Provide practical examples of how to apply the model. Clarify expectations with innovation configuration maps, etc. Support ongoing professional learning. Support ongoing peer coaching and collaboration.	
Not buying into the vision *Stakeholders may feel the model conflicts with their ideals and beliefs about teaching and learning—they don't understand or share the big picture vision or moral purpose for the change.*	Engage people in sharing their moral purpose. Show how the model aligns with ideals and beliefs. Engage in dialogue about how the model will support better outcomes for kids. Provide a clear, compelling picture for how things will be better with the model in place.	
Feeling socially unsafe *Stakeholders may fear or sense that the change conflicts with existing group norms, disrupts social harmony, upends their own social status, or otherwise leaves them feeling socially uncertain and unsafe.*	Share that peer coaching will enhance professionalism. If necessary, call out existing, counterproductive norms. Articulate new norms for collegiality, etc. Show how new norms will improve everyone's practice and make things better.	

Chapter 6: Measuring progress toward success

Angela and Robert, who student-taught together but now teach at different schools on opposite sides of town, meet as promised, right after summer break. School culture issues at Angela's school haven't improved; many teachers are still openly hostile about their principal, Barbara, "forcing" them to use an instructional model. Nonetheless, Angela has quietly decided to use the instructional model in her own classroom and is excited with the headway she is making with her students who struggle most. For example, she tried a few new techniques to help her students better picture the process of photosynthesis. Whereas before she had lectured, shown videos, and created handouts with drawings of the process, this time she had them create skits with students acting as the plants, chlorophyll, sunlight, carbon dioxide, and oxygen. In another lesson, she had students create a "code" for the parts of speech, then use that code to find mistakes in their writing. (She laughed at the memory of how ardently they reminded each other to never end sentences with "purple stars"—better known as prepositions.) Both of these activities fell under her classroom look-fors of visual learning and active engagement.

She's been sharing her new methods and observations with Barbara and a few other trusted peers. Before break, she and Robert had exchanged "LOL" text messages about how she felt she was in some sort of "secret society" that was covertly using the instructional model in their classrooms unbeknownst to the majority bloc who opposed the model. Some parents, likely riled up by angry teachers, had even joined the faculty in expressing displeasure with the new instructional model and with Barbara's leadership, often to a ridiculous degree—for example, accusing Barbara of foisting "unprofessional learning" on teachers. Meanwhile, Angela and her small "club" were energized by seeing the benefits of the model for student learning—something that would no doubt been seen as heresy if they were to bring it up in a faculty meeting.

Over coffee, Angela and Robert compare notes on the striking similarities between the instructional models they've been using in their classrooms. Because they find they're speaking the same language (with only slightly different "accents"), they're able to share which teaching strategies have really resonated with students, places where they're still working to improve their teaching repertoire, and how they are beginning to improvise with proven techniques. "I feel like my 'teacher toolkit' has expanded so much this year!" Angela shares.

Robert nods in agreement. "Right? I looked at my student growth from my first three years in the classroom and I can clearly see a marked difference. Students I probably lost in the past are now doing much better—I think because my lessons aren't 'one and done' anymore—you know, drop the mic and go. Now they're more circular. I'm doing a lot more checks for understanding and have more ways to help kids learn when they don't get it."

Robert adds that his principal, Julia, has been sharing data with them that show similar changes are happening across the school, including some impressive gains in common formative assessment data. "It's really cool," Robert says. "It feels like being on a winning team." Robert adds that the results were significant enough to catch the district's attention; their school was going to be featured in the next district newsletter. "I think we might even talk to the newspaper about it," he adds.

Angela furrows her brow. "You know, we don't even *look* at data at our school," she observes.

"Maybe that's part of the problem. It's kind of like being a ship in a fog, not sure if we're moving forward or drifting backward in the current."

"We're total data geeks," Robert replies. "I give my principal Julia credit for that. We look at data every meeting, but she doesn't make it scary. It's never about who's screwing up or doing something wrong, but how we can get better."

"That sounds nice," Angela says.

"It is. And you know what? I think it's helped to bring people along. We had our own secret society—of people not using the model. But I think the data has made some of the holdouts say, 'Well, maybe there is something to this,' and get on board." ~

What you measure is what you get

Data is the lifeblood of any change effort; without it, it's impossible to track progress or make course corrections. So, as you embark on your current effort to implement an instructional model, it's important to identify what data you'll track, how you'll collect it, how regularly you'll review it, and perhaps most important, your desired endpoint. In short, how will you know when you've been successful?

In this chapter, we'll help you work with your R&I Team to set goals, develop indicators for tracking progress toward your goals, ensure a tight logic between your goals and activities, and (perhaps most importantly) help you create an environment where people readily use data to reflect on their own practices and guide change. As we'll see, this often is something that schools (and companies for that matter) struggle to do well—not from a lack of data (most are awash in data), but rather, because they haven't developed the conditions, attitudes, and cultural norms for using data to examine their own practices honestly and identify real opportunities for improvement.

Begin with a logic model

Before plunging into goal setting, we encourage you to step back for a moment to examine your assumptions—or the logic behind—what you're setting out to do and what you expect to happen as a result. Any action plan comes with a set of implied assumptions: If we do X, then we expect Y to happen. Often, there's a step or two between your actions and desired outcomes (e.g., doing X will make Y better and result in Z).

At its simplest level, it's likely that the logic for implementing an instructional model in your school looks something like this:

Using an instructional model → **Will improve the quality and consistency of student learning experiences** → **Resulting in better student engagement and learning**

That's very basic and superficial, of course. No doubt, your school or district has much more specific outcomes you're hoping to accomplish (such as an instructional model). In the following sections, we'll help you determine how to measure those outcomes so you can convince yourselves and others that things are getting better: How do we know students are more engaged and learning more? We'll also help you to define *what exactly* you hope to see in classrooms to determine that the quality and consistency of student learning experiences are improving: Are lessons more organized? Do they have a better flow? Are students more on task? Finally—moving from right to left (back mapping as it were)—we'll clarify what it will mean for teachers to *use* your instructional model.

For now, though, before getting into the weeds of trying to quantify and measure all of this, we encourage you to stay at a high level, simply examining your basic logic. At this point, you want to consider the *input* (using an instructional model) that you're hoping will lead to new *outputs* (better lessons and learning experiences) and result in a desired *outcome* (better learning). In the box below, we define each of these terms more specifically along with some tips for thinking about and capturing them in a logic model. We all know what people say about assuming, so basically, what you're doing here is making your assumptions explicit so you can check (and recheck) your logic.

> ## Basic elements of logic models
>
> ▸ **Outcomes.** We encourage you to start with these by considering what, ultimately, you want to see happen as a result of all your efforts. As these are your desired outcomes, you may find it helpful to start these with the sentence stem, "We want to . . ."
>
> ▸ **Outputs.** Once you've identified your desired outcomes, you can identify what conditions must be in place to create them. For example, if student engagement is the outcome, what condition (e.g., inquiry-driven learning) are you hoping to create to make this happen? Here, you may find it helpful to start with the sentence stem, "We need to see . . ."
>
> ▸ **Inputs.** Once you know your outcomes and outputs, you can make explicit what exactly you'll do to create the outputs (and outcomes). For example, if engagement is your outcome and inquiry-driven learning your output, your input may be to support teacher professional learning in classroom questions. Here, you may find it helpful to start with the sentence stem, "We will . . ."

Making these assumptions visible may reveal gaps, holes, or flaws in your logic. For example, you may realize that you (or others) are expecting a set of *outcomes* (e.g., developing student critical thinking skills) that are unrelated to your *outputs* (e.g., focusing on learning objectives). So, by first identifying your desired outcomes, then back mapping your outputs and inputs from those—developing your logic model from right (outcomes) to left (inputs)—you can ensure tighter alignment among all three.

Also, because the key idea here is to make your thinking and logic visible, we encourage you not to make this model overly complicated, which can obfuscate the simple logic you're hoping to bring to the fore. If your logic model winds up looking like a stereo wiring diagram, you've probably overdone it and would benefit from paring it down to just the most important, key elements. To illustrate (and to stimulate your thinking), we provide you with an example logic model.

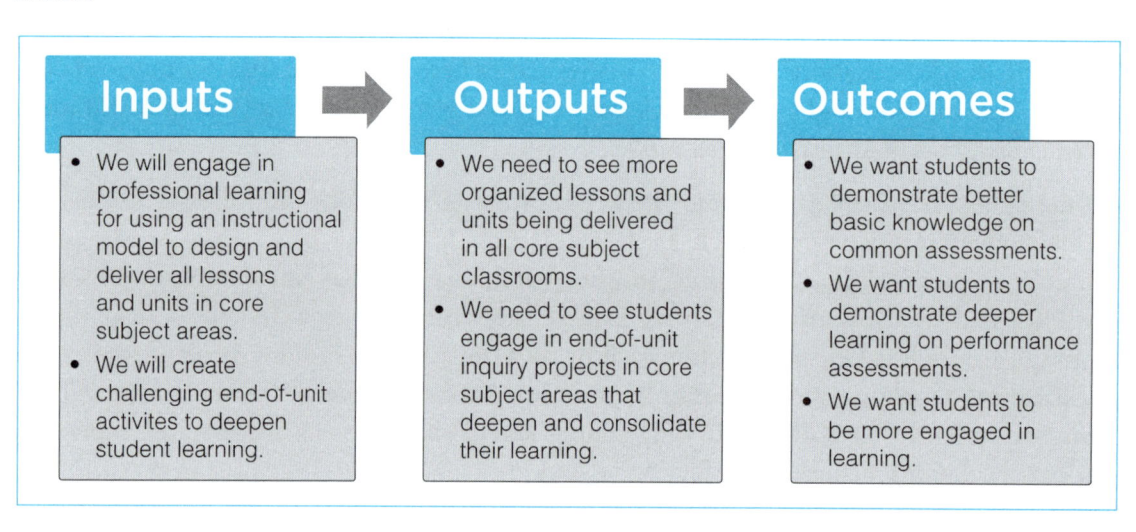

Inputs	Outputs	Outcomes
• We will engage in professional learning for using an instructional model to design and deliver all lessons and units in core subject areas. • We will create challenging end-of-unit activites to deepen student learning.	• We need to see more organized lessons and units being delivered in all core subject classrooms. • We need to see students engage in end-of-unit inquiry projects in core subject areas that deepen and consolidate their learning.	• We want students to demonstrate better basic knowledge on common assessments. • We want students to demonstrate deeper learning on performance assessments. • We want students to be more engaged in learning.

You'll notice that we haven't included any quantifiable measures in this example—that comes later. Right now, the key idea is to make your logic explicit so you can ask yourself: Will our inputs lead to the outputs we believe are necessary to generate our desired outcomes? Again, we encourage you to actually work backwards, starting with your desired outcomes, then identifying what you would need to see in classrooms to make that happen, and what initial activities (or inputs) would drive those outputs. We provide space in Tool 11 on pp. 90–91 for designing your own logic model.

Develop meaningful goals (*outcomes*)

Now that you've identified your desired outcomes in a general way, you're ready to make them more specific and quantifiable. As it turns out, this is one of the most important things you can do as a school leader—set a small number of agreed-upon goals that provide focus, direction, and clarity while still being aspirational enough to inspire and motivate people to stretch themselves to achieve more than they originally thought possible. Years ago, in fact, a McREL research team (2005) found that two key characteristics that separated high-needs, high-performing "beat-the-odds" schools from their lower performing counterparts were 1) an *academic press for achievement* (i.e., high expectations for all students) and 2) *shared mission and goals* (i.e., a clear focus for improvement efforts and resources). Basically, higher-performing schools establish and articulate clear goals for learning and then focus everyone's energies and resources on achieving those goals. Studies of effective school leaders show the same thing: They use challenging goals and performance targets to focus people on doing what matters most—and only what matters most (Public Impact, 2007).

For you, what matters right now, of course, is ensuring consistent use of the instructional model. So you and the other members of your R&I Team will need to consider what goals you'll set to keep everyone clear about your focus. Basically, how will you know when you've been successful? At this point, we encourage you to use the tried-and-true method of setting a S.M.A.R.T (Specific, Measurable, Achievable, Relevant, Time-bound) goal, as explained below.

Setting S.M.A.R.T Goals

Specific: What exactly do you want to see happen?

Measurable: What metric will you use to know when you meet your goal?

Achievable: Is the goal challenging yet attainable?

Relevant: Is it meaningful? Will accomplishing it fulfill your moral purpose?

Time-bound: By which date will you meet your goal?

Here's how, in more specific terms, you might think about these elements with respect to implementing an instructional model.

- **Specific**. Fast forward to the end of your timeline (which you'll define in your Logic Model at the end of this chapter). What would be cause for celebration? What would teachers be doing? What would students be doing?

- **Measurable**. What metric(s) and outcome(s) would tell you, with some degree of certainty, that things have actually gotten better?

- **Achievable**. What would be "game-changing" (worthy of your time and attention) yet do-able? Optimistically, what can you picture getting done with the resources at your disposal? Your goal probably shouldn't be *perfection* (e.g., all students reading at grade level) but rather, some level of *noticeable improvement*.

- **Relevant**. How will you reflect your deeper moral purpose in your goal? After all, the problem you've set out to solve wasn't to implement an instructional model, but to achieve more consistent, high-quality instruction, and ultimately, greater success.

- **Time-bound**. Schools often default to setting goals on a timeline of one school year—usually as an annual school improvement plan. A one-year timeline, however, may be both too *short* and too *long*. Real change in schools often takes two to four years, so one year may be too short to see substantive change, especially when taking an implementation dip into account. On the other hand, it can be difficult to maintain a sense of urgency when pursuing a goal that stretches over a year, so you may decide to set shorter-term (e.g., one quarter, trimester, or semester) goals.

We encourage you to consider multiple outcomes beyond summative test scores. Are students more engaged/less distracted during lessons? Have absenteeism or behavior referrals dropped? All of these can be powerful indicators that students are finding meaning in the work they are doing in the classroom. Moreover, these outcomes may show up long before you see any significant movement in test scores, particularly with standardized tests. To stimulate your thinking, here are some example S.M.A.R.T goals for desired *outcomes* of implementing an instructional model.

- *By the end of the first semester, we want to see 80% of students surveyed agreeing with the statement, "I believe I can achieve my personal learning goals."*
- *By the end of the trimester, we want to see 75% of students performing at grade level on common formative assessments.*
- *By the end of the year, we want to see disciplinary referrals drop by 50%.*

Identify leading indicators (*outputs*)

Now that you've achieved more clarity about your desired outcomes, you can consider what changes in classroom conditions will lead to those outcomes. Here, you're seeking to determine more than just simply what you'll *do*, but how you'll influence your outcomes with factors that remain *under your control*. For example, if you've identified "student mastery of foundational concepts" as a desired outcome, you might specify "ideal use of checks for understanding and feedback" as a key output for achieving that outcome—harkening back to the innovation configuration map you've created for that particular phase of your instructional model.

Another way to think of outputs is that they're *leading* indicators, whereas student outcomes are *lagging* indicators. Often, it can take a year or even more to see significant changes on standardized achievement tests, so it's important to consider what changes might be observable in relatively short order—in classrooms, student engagement surveys, or classroom-based assessments—that would suggest improvements in student performance are on the way. In short, you're asking yourselves: What do we need to observe in classrooms to know we're creating the right conditions for student success? To answer this question, you may need to track data from classroom "look-fors," student surveys or interviews, or common formative assessments.

Here are some examples:

- *By the end of the semester, we need to see all lesson and unit plans reflecting our instructional design model.*
- *By the end of the quarter, we need to see "ideal" levels of use on our rubric for the "students consolidate and reflect on their learning" phase of learning in 80% of classroom observations.*
- *By the end of the year, we need to see 75% of students (up from 50%) reporting, "My teacher makes our learning goals clear for each lesson."*
- *When asked, 80% of students can articulate in their own words what the overall learning objective is for a given lesson.*

If you don't already have obvious ways to measure these outputs, that's OK. We'll provide you with some guidance for creating these measures later. For now, let's consider the final link in your chain of logic: What exactly you'll *do* to create these desired outputs—that is, the *inputs* of your logic model.

Identify focused activities (*inputs*)

At this point, you're ready to connect dots, drawing a straight line from what you want to see happen for students (your desired *outcomes*) to what conditions you need to see in classrooms (your *outputs*). To achieve your desired outcomes, what precisely will you do to start this chain of events—that is, what supports you'll provide teachers to encourage classroom conditions to change? Asking this is apt to help you clarify and focus your activities. For example, you're likely to see that saying, "We'll provide PL in the instructional model" is probably too vague if your desired outcome is "By the end of the first semester, 80% of students surveyed will agree with the statement, 'I believe I can achieve my personal learning goals'" or if you're expecting to see consistent use of student-developed learning goals in classrooms. Thus, you'll want to ensure your professional learning and ongoing supports for teachers are sufficiently focused and robust to, in this case, help teachers (and students) develop and track their own progress toward learning goals.

Herein lies the power of logic models. By making our assumptions explicit at each step along the way, we can see when our assumptions don't add up—when, in effect, we're hoping two and two will add up to five. When we detect this happening, we must better focus our activities (*inputs*) to create the conditions (*outputs*) necessary to achieve our goals. Conversely, we may see that our desired outcomes (*goals*) are simply too ambitious and should be scaled back to avoid setting ourselves up for failure and disappointment.

Capturing your activities as inputs in your logic model can help you to avoid wishful thinking by considering what's actually reasonable: How many days of professional learning can you incorporate into your school calendar (how much will teachers tolerate and/or be able to absorb)? Given time constraints, where will you focus your professional learning (and teacher coaching) efforts? How much new "stuff" (rewriting lesson and unit plans, designing project-based learning assignments, developing higher-order questions, etc.) can teachers reasonably be expected to do in the time allotted?

As you do this, you'll want to check your logic: Do our professional learning activities align with the conditions you need to see in classrooms? Are we giving teachers enough opportunities to learn the model and adequate time to apply it in reshaping their classroom practices? If teachers do what we're asking them to do, will classroom conditions change in the ways we've specified in our output statements?

Here, you may find it helpful to use the sentence stem "We will . . ." followed by an action verb, as shown in the following examples:

- *Prior to the start of the school year, we will provide teacher professional learning on the instructional model with special emphasis on (and innovation configuration maps for) student goal setting.*

- *During the first quarter, we will ensure peer coaching triads commit to developing "ideal" use of student goal setting in classrooms.*

- *Over the summer, working together as teacher teams, we will design and develop new lesson and unit plans that follow the instructional model.*

- *Prior to the semester, we will develop examples of higher-order questions in all subject areas and grades to support "ideal" use of questioning strategies during the "guide new learning" phase of the model.*

The key point here is that you want to be clear and concrete about what exactly you as an R&I Team and your teachers will commit to doing together (remember, you're all in this together!) to ensure everyone involved can effectively apply the instructional model to create the sorts of classroom conditions you've already identified and agreed are critical for student success.

Finding (or creating) the right tools for measuring progress

As you've considered your outputs and outcomes (and read some of the examples provided here), you may have had no problem envisioning how you could collect and report data in real time to track your progress toward them. Maybe you already have tools and/or protocols for surveying students, observing classrooms on a regular basis, and monitoring student academic progress (e.g., on a benchmark or common classroom assessments). If, however, you don't have these data at your fingertips, that's OK. As it turns out, there are several fairly simple ways you can collect these data, which is far better, of course, than simply deciding, *Well, we don't have those data handy, so we just won't track that*—which is a bit like flying a plane without an altimeter or driving a car without a speedometer.

Developing and tracking classroom look-fors

In your logic model, you've likely identified some changes you need to see in classrooms (your *outputs*). If you haven't already, you should consider what exactly you need to *see* to know these new conditions are in place. For example, if you're focused on ensuring students use and understand success criteria, teachers might agree to implement student "turn and talks" at the start of lessons to clarify the learning objective and then, as a check for understanding, call on a handful of students to restate the success criteria in their own words. That's an *input*. The *output* is that students are clearer about their success criteria.

To measure this, observers could quietly ask a few students what the success criteria are for a lesson or unit and tally up the percentage of students who are able to articulate the criteria clearly. In addition, if teachers have agreed to make success criteria visible for every lesson, observers could also tally up (and aggregate) how often they see success criteria made visible for students in the classrooms they visit. In so doing, they could measure both inputs and outputs in fairly brief (5–7 minutes) visits to classrooms and help everyone connect the dots between their inputs and outputs. Revisit the guidance we gave on instructional rounds on p. 20. The same tips and tools can be adapted for use here.

In this case, teachers might see that when they take the time to ensure their classes understand their success criteria, most students are able to articulate, when asked, what they were learning and why. For example, during a lesson on photosynthesis, when asked about the purpose of a group drawing activity to illustrate the photosynthesis process, students might answer, "Well, drawing the process and talking about it helps us better understand what's happening in the air, soil, and the plant as it makes food." Conversely, when teachers don't take the time to clarify learning objectives, observers may hear students say, "Because it's what my teacher asked me to do" when asked why they're engaged in a particular learning activity. So, by observing and reporting data regularly during classroom visits, teachers and peer coaches, working together, can see progress in student engagement and learning as a result of their efforts to get students to consider success criteria at the start of a lesson.

So, the key message here is that measures of classroom activities need not be complex, but simple and focused and aligned with the outcomes and outputs you've identified on your logic model. See some examples of classroom look-fors to stimulate your thinking on the next page.

Table 9. Classroom look-fors—Goodwin, *Student Learning That Works* (2018)

Look-fors: How Teacher Guides Learning	The Classroom Toolkit	Example
The teacher actively plans for getting students interested in the topic.	Help students connect emotionally to their learning. Help students begin to ask questions by creating a mystery or suspense.	The teacher begins a discussion of geometry with how students currently feel about math and geometry, and why they might have negative emotions associated with this subject. Prior to a lesson on angles, the teacher brings in a mini pool table and shows how players can anticipate the angle at which a ball will travel given the angle at which it is struck.
The teacher helps students set goals for learning.	Asking essential questions Encouraging personal learning goals	After the billiards demonstration, the teacher has students finish sentence stems: I already have some idea of… I want to know why… I would like to be able to…
The teacher creates multiple avenues for learning new content.	Thought-provoking questions Nonlinguistic representations	Using golf balls, the students break into small groups to further explore how to move a ball in a desired direction by using a cue ball. The teacher then has pairs explain to each other what they think is happening. This is followed by a silent written self-reflection of what they learned during the activity.
The teacher helps students to begin making sense of learning.	Summarizing Clarifying feedback	The students complete diagrams of the direction in which they wanted the ball to go (e.g., 10°) and where it had to be struck (e.g., 190°). They then create short recordings explaining their diagrams.
The teacher provides opportunities for students to practice and rehearse what they have learned.	Practice and reflection	Students complete drawings showing various angles: 45°, 90°, 180°, and 270°. They add labels for acute, right, and obtuse.
The teacher provides activities to help students extend and apply their learning.	Application Personal meaning	Using circular food (pizza, cake, or pie), the small groups must figure out at which angles to slice their dish so that each member of the group gets an equal share.

Common formative assessments

Quite likely, the most important (but not only) data you'll want to track to measure outcomes is related to student learning. Here, you'll want to collect real-time data instead of waiting months for results from large-scale assessments to arrive. It's possible your school or district is already doing this through some form of interim benchmark assessments. These data are helpful, of course. However, you're apt to find that more informal, common formative assessments may be even more effective for tracking student learning. By this, we mean assessment items that teachers develop together and embed in regular classroom routines for the purpose of tracking and sharing student progress and making real-time adjustments to teaching and learning (Hofman, Goodwin, & Kahl, 2015), rather than so-called interim assessments, which are typically commercially developed large-scale standardized achievement tests that are simply administered with greater frequency than statewide assessments.

For example, if you're focused on helping students apply new concepts in novel situations, you might embed the same complex problem in an end-of-unit mathematics assessment across all classrooms in the same grade level. Or if you want to see how deeply students are grasping a particular concept or skill, such as using close reading to identify implicit themes in reading passages, you might collaboratively develop and use the same prompt for extended answers on an assessment of language arts. Ideally, your common formative assessment items would reflect areas that you know from prior (even large-scale) assessments have challenged students. You'll use the results of these assessments to adjust instruction (and reteach critical concepts) as necessary. The point here is that by using common formative assessment data, you'll be collecting and tracking real-time data on the impact of your instructional model on student learning.

One key to consistent assessment and feedback in your classrooms is to calibrate how teachers might score student work. For example, a team of teachers could each bring a student example of a completed assignment that they had each given. As they look at the three anonymous examples for scoring, they individually ask themselves the following questions:

- What are all the criteria that come to mind when I assess this work?
- Of those criteria, which are most crucial for assessing this work? Which are extraneous?
- Would I assess this work differently if I knew the student had a learning difference? Would I assess this work differently if I knew the student was intellectually advanced?
- Given the most crucial criteria, how would I score this example?

This protocol helps to foster discussions of criteria, what's important/not important, and how consistently the teachers assess common assignments.

Student engagement measures

You'll likely also want to measure student engagement. Fortunately, just like student learning, this doesn't need to be a complicated endeavor. Yes, there are scientifically validated instruments for measuring student motivation, engagement, and perspectives on the quality of teaching and learning in the classroom. If you already have one of these, that's great. No doubt, you'll be able to glean useful data from it to track an instructional model's impact on student engagement.

Nonetheless (and even if you already have one of these more sophisticated instruments), you may find you can create and administer simple student surveys that provide you with valuable data to track the impact of your work on student engagement. For example, you might simply ask them questions like these:

- On a scale from 1 to 5 (with 1 being "Not at all" and 5 being "Frequently"), how often do you feel challenged at school?

- On a scale from 1 to 5 (with 1 being "Not at all" and 5 being "Frequently"), how often does your teacher invite you to engage in class discussions?

- On a scale from 1 to 5 (with 1 being "Hardly ever" and 5 being "Nearly all the time"), how clear are you about your success criteria for lessons and units?

- On a scale from 1 to 5 (with 1 being "Hardly ever" and 5 being "Nearly all the time"), how interested are you in what you're learning in class?

The key point here is that these measures need not be overly sophisticated or exhaustive, but rather, a simple check-in—simple enough that it's no big deal to repeat the same survey a few weeks later and you're able to collect data with relatively low-tech methods. If you want to use online surveys or the like, that's fine. You may find they save time when it comes to tabulating data. But you can also use very basic methods like asking students to take anonymous, 3–4 question pencil-and-paper surveys. You just want a quick snapshot of how things are changing for students, so don't over-complicate matters.

Staff climate and culture surveys

You may also identify school climate and culture as yet another important measure. After all, as we've noted earlier, the success of your effort to apply an instructional model in classrooms is likely to hinge on the level of collegiality and sense of shared purpose in your school. So, these are good data to track. Here, you may choose to use a variety of free school climate and culture tools—including the free U.S. Department of Education School Climate Survey (EDSCLS), which is appropriate for grades 5–12 students, staff, and parents—or develop your own short survey.

As with student engagement surveys, do-it-yourself surveys will likely not be as valid or reliable as scientifically validated instruments, so it's best to use these data for formative purposes only. So, if you're going to hold people accountable for these results or report them publicly, we suggest you stick with validated instruments. Here, we'd also suggest that you consider what's known as Campbell's law—named after former president of the American Psychological Association, Donald Campbell, who observed that measures tend to become less accurate the greater the stakes attached to them. So, if you're interested in collecting accurate data to size up what's working and what's not—and make course corrections accordingly—we urge you to refrain from attaching stringent punishments or rewards to these measures.

This brings us to our next discussion: the culture you create in your school around data use.

Creating a culture of data use

Better data drives better decisions, or so we like to think. Yet many schools (like many businesses, it turns out), struggle to use data effectively. For starters, as a recent survey of 4,600 teachers found, teachers are often overwhelmed by *too much* data, so much so that it's difficult to "separate the signal from the noise" (Bill & Melinda Gates Foundation, 2015, p. 18). Moreover, much of this flood of data comes too late, leaving teachers feeling as if they're driving by looking through the rear window. As in-depth studies of schools have found, many teachers have little use for data from standardized reading assessments. As one teacher put it, "A lot of this stuff I could have figured out . . . without the testing"—simply by listening to students while they read (Young, 2006, p. 527). These findings harken back to our refrain in the previous section to keep data simple, classroom-based, and actionable.

Studies have also found that the more complex the data set, the less helpful it is for making adjustments to instruction; one study of 230 teachers presented with "data scenarios" (i.e., asking them to make judgments from data sets) found they often "lost track of what they were trying to figure out . . . if the calculation became at all complicated" (U.S. Department of Education, 2011, p. 61). So, again, we remind you to keep your data sets as simple and straightforward as possible. As is so often the case, less is more.

Using data as a mirror, not a window

At the same time, it's important to develop a school culture that's receptive to using data. For example, an in-depth examination of two middle schools engaged in a mathematics reform—one far more effectively than the other—revealed a tale of two schools when it came to data use (Horn, Kane, & Wilson, 2015). In the lower-performing school, data conversations were mostly superficial, focusing on how to present data differently or predicting how many kids might fall into various performance bands on the upcoming state test, with no reflection on how to improve instruction. Similarly, researchers in Florida and California observed data teams simply going through the motions, whizzing through a data discussion protocol without reflecting or identifying how to improve instruction before exclaiming with relief, "Yay, we're done!" (Datnow, Park, & Kennedy-Lewis, 2013, p. 355).

Case studies of data teams reveal a lot about their attitudes regarding students and schooling. For example, in some schools, conversations about improving student achievement focused mostly on sending "bubble kids" (those whose test results fell just below proficiency cutoffs) to tutoring or afterschool programs (Horn, Kane, & Wilson, 2015, p. 225). In other words, the perceived solution is about what *someone else* might do instead of how teachers could change *their own* instructional practices to boost student learning. In these schools, the shared belief seemed to be that poor student achievement related more to student deficits than teacher shortcomings; in short, the mindset appeared to be, "We're OK; it's our students who are the problem." Even in schools where teachers dug more deeply into student data—for example, taking a close look at problems students had missed to see what concepts they had failed to grasp—their conversations failed to consider alternate ways they might teach the concept. Instead, they pledged to "hit hard" on the concept in the future—doing more of the same and expecting different results (Horn, Kane, & Wilson, 2015, p. 235). In short, many schools seem to use data as a window—something they peer into to see what may be going wrong for others. In contrast, teachers in high-performing schools use data more like a mirror—as a way to reflect on their own practices, respectfully question one another, and identify important adjustments to make.

Creating teacher growth mindsets

The shift in perspective and culture that high-performing schools undergo is no accident, but rather the result of a strong principal or team of leaders who are able to clearly define the purpose of using data (i.e., to guide instructional changes) and create a "we feeling" in the school (Datnow, Park, & Kennedy-Lewis, 2013, p. 353). In particular, these leaders clarify and model norms for data conversations, specifying what materials—and attitudes—teachers should bring to meetings, such as how they should hold one another accountable and argue productively by adopting slogans like, "Whatever happens in your meeting, stays in your meeting," and ensuring conversations about students didn't devolve into "nit-picking or trash talking" (p. 354).

They also seem to recognize that high-pressure environments make it hard for people to own up to their shortcomings and work together. This is exactly what a study of high-stakes accountability in an urban district found: The longer low-performing schools faced the threat of sanctions, the less apt they were to examine underlying assumptions and current practices and pull together to improve them (Finnigan, Daly, & Che, 2012). In short, when teachers fear they will be judged, they are less likely to engage in self-reflection and identify areas for improvement. Unless leadership teams create a safe environment and set a tone akin to what Japanese manufacturers refer to as *kaizen*—the view that "every defect is a treasure" because it points to ways to do things better—teachers can have all the data in the world but do little with them to guide improvement.

As you collect data and share them with teachers, here are a few ways you can ensure people are ready to use these data to guide improvement.

- **Establish norms for data conversations**. These might include keeping the focus on continuous improvement; not judging people but identifying mistakes so that we can avoid *errors* (repeated mistakes); giving everyone a chance to speak and share ideas; engaging in active listening; encouraging dissent; and focusing on teacher practices and factors under our control.

- **Keep asking why**. To ensure you don't settle on easy answers or solutions, encourage everyone to keep digging deeper by engaging in what's sometimes called a 5-Why process, asking repeated why questions to get to the root cause of issues. For example, if students are struggling to engage in analytical work, you might ask, *Why* is that occurring? An initial answer might be because they aren't capable of engaging in close reading. So, you would ask *why* that is occurring, then *why* is that happening, and so on. Ultimately, these questions should lead to everyone identifying, through shared inquiry, what they can do to improve instruction, which brings us to our next point.

- **Focus on teaching, learning, and classroom conditions, not student deficits**. Data conversations should help teachers develop a sense of collective efficacy—the belief that, together, they can help students succeed. So, it's important to avoid blaming students, as that takes control *out of* teachers' hands. Conversations should continually bend back toward the question, What can we do about what these data are telling us? As you do this, be sure to keep conversations focused on teaching *practices*, not teachers. For example, instead of saying, "Too many teachers aren't doing XYZ" (which is apt to make people defensive), say, "We need to increase the frequency of XYZ in classrooms."

- **Build on your strengths.** Don't overlook the bright spots in your data—places, for example, where students are engaged, where the instructional model is having a positive impact, and teachers are having breakthroughs with students. After all, the solutions lie in what's going right, not in what's going wrong.

Thinking like researchers and scientists

Ultimately, your data conversations will be productive when people approach them with an *experimental*, not a compliance-oriented, mindset. That's one of the benefits of developing logic models; they help you to develop and test hypotheses for how to improve student learning (e.g., if we apply an instructional model in every classroom, we'll ensure greater consistency and quality of instruction). Like researchers or scientists, you're collecting data to see if your hypothesis is correct and engaging in honest inquiry, which requires ensuring teachers feel safe to try new methods and to acknowledge mistakes and gaps in knowledge. Here are some questions you might ask to encourage an experimental mindset:

- What do we expect to get better when we use a model with greater consistency?
- How will we know if we're following the model well?
- What data points would change?
- What might we observe in six weeks? A semester? A school year?
- What learning do we need to do together to reduce variance?

In many ways, these questions reflect the key tenets of what Bryk, Gomez, Grunow, & LeMahieu (2015) called "improvement science." This is an approach to implementation that starts with a clear understanding of the problem at hand from a user's perspective (e.g., what are learning experiences like for students?), focuses on variations in performance as the core problem to address (e.g., variability in student experiences across classrooms), considers how the current design of the system contributes to those variances (e.g., teachers following different instructional models or none at all), and accelerates improvements by encouraging people to work together in networks.

Data team meeting protocol

As teams come together the first few times to discuss student learning, it helps to lay a few ground rules so that members feel safe from blame or criticism. Encourage them to think of themselves as learning scientists who are analyzing what works in instruction.

Agreements:

The 4th-grade data team agrees to:

- Recognize bright spots in teaching in each of our meetings.
- Bring concerns about student learning to the table in a way that is caring and nonthreatening.
- Brainstorm together for solutions to learning challenges.
- Offer support to our colleagues in a way that respects the profession.

Final reflection and checklist

Here are some questions to reflect on as a school or district-level R&I Team and a checklist for guiding implementation.

Reflecting together

- Do we have shared understanding and buy-in of our desired outcomes?
- Are we clear about the logic of our efforts—how what we'll do (inputs) will change classroom conditions (outputs) and improve student engagement and learning (outcomes)?
- What existing data and tools can we use to track the impact of our efforts?
- What new tools or data collection methods might we need to develop and use to track our efforts?
- How would we characterize our school culture when it comes to data use? Do we currently use data as a window (seeing what others are doing wrong) or a mirror (reflecting on what we can do better)? What could we do to ensure we use data as a mirror?

Checklist for measuring progress and impact

- ☐ Identify your goals (what you want to see/outcomes) for student engagement, learning, school culture, etc.
- ☐ Identify the conditions that need to be in place (what you need to see/outputs) to achieve your goals.
- ☐ Identify how you'll support these new conditions as an R&I Team (what you will do/inputs), including what professional learning, resources, coaching, and leadership you'll provide.
- ☐ Connect these dots with a logic model, using Tool 11.
- ☐ Review your logic model for gaps and non sequiturs.
- ☐ Develop norms and agreements for data team meetings to encourage a "kaizen" approach to data.

Check out
Chapter 6 Tools
on the following pages

Tool 11: Creating a logic model

A logic model can help you plan for resources, activities (inputs), and expected outputs and outcomes of your new model. Use the tool below to capture your plan for success.

Inputs	Outputs	
What resources are provided?	Activities	Who will implement

Outcomes

Short-term	Long-term

Chapter 7: Building on your foundation

Fast forward through time. It's the end of the school year—two years after Julia's school first embarked on implementing an instructional model. She's sitting down with Robert for his last one-on-one meeting of the year. Robert shares how much he has grown professionally in this, his fifth year in the classroom and second full year using the instructional model—particularly how much the instructional model has helped him pull disparate strategies together into a more cohesive mental model for structuring student learning. He confesses that at first, his use of the model felt a bit stiff and uncomfortable, like a new pair of shoes. But now that the shoes are fully "broken in" and the model's cadence is coming naturally to him, he's finding it easier to plan lessons and units and share lessons with colleagues. Even his students are more attuned to their own learning and his instruction, asking him to reteach in different ways when they struggle at first to grasp a concept or develop a skill.

Across the school, the onboarding plan for new teachers and peer mentoring for all teachers seems to have paid off; most newer teachers are up to speed on the instructional model and apply it consistently in their classrooms. They also have the benefit of what Robert describes as a "treasure trove" of great lessons to use in their classrooms. Best of all, Robert's regular touchpoints with his grade-level team have become less about upcoming events or grousing about kids; instead, they're deep dives into student artifacts and sharing teaching strategies that show promise. To cap off an amazing year, Julia has just asked him to become the grade level lead for the next year.

"I'm super excited about being a grade level lead," he adds. "But I do have a question: Are we still focusing on the model next year?"

Julia nods. "Yes. Why do you ask?"

Robert shrugs. "Well, over spring break, I started reading a lot about students in trauma, which got me to wondering if focusing just on instruction is maybe too narrow, like maybe we ought to be, you know, expanding our programming a bit."

Julia ponders Robert's question, then asks, "So, what kinds of things have you been learning about?"

"Well, like how kids who have experienced trauma have a hard time focusing in class and trusting others," Robert says, then sighs softly. "You know, I was actually one of those kids. My dad's 10 years sober now but had a drinking problem when I was a kid. And he was a mean, violent drunk. I know what it's like to be sitting in class, feeling on edge with your head somewhere else. So, I guess I'm just feeling like I'm teaching better than I've ever been, but it's still not enough."

"So, what do you have in mind?" Julia asks, her face earnest as she awaits Robert's reply.

He pauses. "I don't know. I'm not saying abandon the model by any means. Maybe I just want to be sure we don't get stuck on one thing—an instructional model—as the be-all-end-all."

"So, does anything you're reading about trauma-informed practices contradict what we're doing with our teaching model?"

Robert shakes his head. "No, not really. If anything, it probably just puts a finer point on things, like creating a safe and supportive environment for learning and then really drawing kids into the lesson and giving them time to process what they're learning."

Julia thinks for a moment. "So, what if we did this . . . how would you like to head a task force to look at trauma-informed practice and come back with a short list of recommendations for how we can infuse those practices into our instructional model?"

"I'd like that," Robert replies. "It's kind of like we're saying the instructional model is our computer operating system on which we run new programs and apps." He smiles as he leaves the meeting. His conversation with Julia has a familiar ring to it and he can't wait to dive in. ~

Taking next steps with your instructional model

Ultimately, you'll likely reach a point where your instructional model becomes so ingrained in classrooms that it no longer requires such intense focus to ensure consistent, ideal use of the various components of the model. Of course, even at this point, it's important to remind staff periodically that just because you're not devoting every professional learning opportunity to the model or discussing it in every faculty meeting doesn't mean you don't expect everyone to keep using it to guide instruction.

In fact, because improvement is a journey, you should never assume that once your instructional model is in place, you can simply set it and forget it. Instead, you're more likely to follow one of these paths forward:

- **Adapting your model**. You may find you need to make tweaks to your model to support your students or capture new understandings about teaching and learning, creating in effect, a "version 2.0" of your instructional model.
- **Enhancing your model**. Similar to adapting your model, you may find ways to leave the model essentially unchanged, but integrate new ideas, methods, and approaches into it.
- **Developing expertise with your model**. Ideally, your model should serve as a springboard for developing teaching expertise and unleashing innovation.
- **Replacing your model**. In rare circumstances, you may find that your chosen model is simply unworkable or not helping to address student learning needs, so you need to select a different one.

We'll describe each of these options in a bit more detail in the following sections.

Adapting your model

Case studies of schools that engage in continuous improvement—boosting student performance not just for a few years, but over the long term—find that these schools often reflect an *adopt, then adapt* approach to improvement. That is, a few years after adopting, for example, an off-the-shelf curriculum, they observed (using data) that while their chosen program was an improvement over previous practices, which were largely inconsistent and idiosyncratic, their adopted program wasn't yet perfect, so they began to *adapt* it to better meet student needs. Yet they were careful not to revert back to inconsistency; instead, everyone understood that changes to the program would be universal, creating what in effect became a new version of the same consistent model—akin to software or smartphone manufacturers creating a "version 2.0" of their product.

Here are a few questions that might help you to consider whether this is the right path for your school:

- Are there any situations (e.g., particular classes, subject areas, or student groups) in which the model doesn't appear to be working? And are we convinced the *model itself* is ineffective—and not simply being implemented ineffectively?
- Have we noticed any *positive* deviations in our use of the model—that is, places where teachers have made changes or tweaks in the design and/or delivery of instruction and are getting better outcomes as a result?
- Do we find ourselves stumbling over words, concepts, or strategies that simple reframing might address?
- Are there parts of our instructional model that are too vague or too complex?
- Do we need to add or remove anything from our model to ensure mastery learning?

Enhancing your model

As we noted at the outset of this book, schools often have a tendency to add more "stuff" to what they're doing, hoping (falsely) that doing more will make them better. So much frenetic activity, noted a team of researchers observing one particular school in Chicago, may dazzle onlookers, like "a Christmas tree laden with ornaments dazzles a child" (Bryk, Sebring, Kerbow, Rollow, & Easton, 1998, p. 115), yet the relentless pursuit of more does little to "strengthen… the core of the school" and can leave a school sagging under "the weight of all the ornaments" with its trunk "withering" and roots "dry."

As your instructional model becomes more consistent in classrooms, you're apt to find you have more bandwidth to consider other levers for improvement, such as re-examining your curriculum to ensure it supports deep learning or considering non-academic supports for student success. As you consider these other levers, we'd encourage you to look for ways that your current instructional model might serve as a platform for running a new program so teachers don't feel you're dumping one more thing on them.

Consider, for example, Response to Intervention (RTI), alternatively called Multi-Tiered System of Supports (MTSS). Such an approach ought to build on the "best first instruction" provided through the instructional model, by identifying ways to repeat or focus more heavily on some phases of the instructional model for students who struggle to master particular concepts or skills. Similarly, you might identify ways to infuse social emotional learning into your model by, for example, helping students develop emotional readiness during the "launch" phase of your model, growth mindsets during the goal-setting phase, and empathy during the sense-making (i.e., cooperative learning) phase. Similarly, any new educational technology solution ought to be explicitly framed as helping to enhance teachers' use of the instructional model.

So, to ensure coherence and avoid initiative overload (i.e., putting too many ornaments on your tree), here are questions to contemplate as you consider additional initiatives beyond your instructional model:

- How might we accomplish [fill in the blank] through our current instructional model?
- Will this new [program/initiative/directive] align with our current instructional model? If not, is it still worth pursuing? How will we explain the contradiction to teachers?
- If we are purchasing a new program or solution, can the vendor show how it aligns with, or supports better use of, our current instructional model? If not, is it worth purchasing?

See Tool 12 on p. 99 for an example of infusing MTSS practices with existing instructional model practices.

Building on your model to develop expertise and unleash innovation

As we've noted earlier, a common objection to instructional models is that they can become limiting or stifle teacher creativity and development. This is a risk especially if leaders insist that teachers follow the model in a scripted, didactic, or superficial way. Following a model is often an important *first phase* to developing talent and expertise. Thus, when it comes to teachers developing their talents, a model is a means to an end, not an end in itself. Yes, you want teachers to follow the model, but more importantly, you want them to understand *why* it works and then to develop and bring a robust repertoire of teaching strategies to each phase of the model, continually considering which strategies work best in which situations.

Madeline Hunter, creator of a prominent instructional model, herself noted that what's most important is not that anyone blindly follow her model, but that they develop "propositional knowledge," or knowing what "affects student learning" so they can make sound professional decisions when designing and delivering lessons (Hunter, 1985, p. 57). Thus, she insisted that an instructional model shouldn't stifle creativity or professionalism, but rather, "provide the launching pad from which [teacher] creativity can soar" (p. 58). With this in mind, she cautioned against administrators applying rigid interpretations of the model, including using it as an evaluation tool, insisting that every lesson include every element, and most egregiously, judging teachers' use of the model without first asking them for their rationale in using a particular strategy. Indeed, one of the most important outcomes of applying an instructional model ought to be teachers developing increasing understanding of *why* they are applying particular strategies during particular phases of learning.

So, as you reach a point where use of the model is becoming increasingly consistent—dare we say *automatic*—in the classroom, you're apt to face a new challenge: ensuring that teachers are *intentional* in their use of the model and not simply following it in a rote, simplistic, or mindless way—for example, engaging in "I do, we do, you do" ad nauseum without considering ways to enhance a sequence of learning (e.g., engaging students in productive struggle by inverting the sequence). Similarly, you'll want to ensure that as school leaders, you don't fall into the trap of looking for superficial trappings of the instructional model without considering (or asking teachers to reflect on) the *why* behind the *what*.

Remember, your ultimate goal in applying an instructional model in your classrooms is to ensure greater consistency *and* quality of instruction. Quality only comes about when teachers are intentional about their practice, continually reflecting on why they're doing what they're doing, evaluating whether it's working, and considering if there might be better ways to guide student learning. If (and only if) these conditions are present, can teachers use an instructional model, in Hunter's words, as a "launching pad" for creativity and, ultimately, innovation. Here are some questions for you to consider as an R&I Team to ensure your instructional model doesn't get stuck at a rudimentary level of implementation:

- Have we articulated the *why* for the *what* of our instructional model? Do we know (and have we shared) the "propositional knowledge" or "theories of actions" that underpin the model?
- Do our teachers understand the *why* behind our instructional model?
- Do teacher coaches and instructional leaders consistently ask teachers to share their logic or rationale for the professional choices they're making in the classroom?
- Do we create regular opportunities for teachers to engage in rich professional dialogue, sharing not only what's working but *why* it's working?
- Do we celebrate and share new, innovative strategies for delivering the instructional model?

You can find additional reflective questions in Tool 13 on p. 100.

Replacing your model

While uncommon, in some circumstances, you might find that after two to three years of concerted effort to apply an instructional model in classrooms, it simply hasn't had the impact you expected. Thus, it may be time to consider abandoning the model. The first question to ask here, of course, is whether the model itself or poor implementation is at fault. If your data and classroom observations suggest that teachers simply aren't using the model, you might ask if you need to reconsider your approach to leadership (by revisiting chapter 5). In doing so, you might consider if you've provided adequate professional learning opportunities for teachers— or if perhaps the model is simply too complex or unwieldy to implement well, or alternatively, too simplistic to reflect the level of sophistication or capacity of your teachers. Or perhaps too many teachers understand what to do, but not *why* to do it, and are thus using the model in overly simplistic ways.

Alternatively, if you're convinced you've implemented the model consistently, with "ideal" level of use in most classrooms, then it's possible the model is somehow a mismatch for your students' needs or that it reflects an entirely different approach to instructional design than your chosen curriculum. This could be the case if you're attempting to follow a prescribed math or reading program. In either case, once you feel you have truly given the model a fair chance of success and do not see improvement, you and your R&I Team will need to consider trying a different one. We place special emphasis on trying a *different* model here (as opposed to altogether abandoning the idea of having an instructional model) for the reasons we laid out in chapter 1: namely, that having an instructional model—one well suited to your students and teachers—is a critical leverage point for improving the quality and consistency of instruction in your schools and classrooms.

If you feel you've reached this point of needing to replace your model with a different one, here are a few questions you might ask.

- How much is poor implementation versus poor model fit at fault for our lack of results? Why, specifically, do we think that?
- What will we do to ensure we're more successful in our efforts next time?
- Did we miss any important steps in how we selected or rolled out our instructional model last time that we need to be sure to engage in this time?

Final reflection and checklist

Here are some questions to reflect on as a school or district-level R&I Team and a checklist for considering next steps with your model.

Reflecting together

- Where are we with our model? Do we need to adapt, enhance, build deeper expertise, or select a new model?
- What has gone well to date with our efforts? What bright spots should we celebrate?
- What have we learned as an R&I Team about this work—about implementing complex change initiatives that require teachers to change their habits?
- What evidence do we see of teachers sharing a common language and having common understandings of the *what* and *why* of the model?
- Have we been adequately focused on implementing the instructional model? Or did we have too many "ornaments on the tree"?
- What might cause us to lose focus on the model? What will we do to prevent that from happening? What will we do if we feel it *is* happening?

Checklist for building on your foundation

- ☐ Identify any potential *adaptations* of your instructional model that might improve effectiveness or implementation.
- ☐ Identify ways to integrate new change initiatives as *enhancements* for your instructional model, using Tool 12.
- ☐ Clarify and articulate (if you haven't already done so) the theories of action or propositional knowledge underlying your instructional model.
- ☐ Engage teachers in dialogue about the what and *why* of the model, using Tool 13.
- ☐ Provide teachers with a road map for what comes next.

Check out *Chapter 7 Tools* on the following pages

Tool 12: Cross-referencing current models with new initiatives

When thinking about how to overlay new practices with your instructional model, you may find it helpful to create a matrix showing where the two concepts overlap. Below is an example of integrating new trauma-informed procedures with existing processes. Note that Robert designates which practices will overlap especially with Tier 2 and Tier 3 students, drawing from Multi-Tiered Systems of Support (MTSS). In this model, Tier 1 practices are those administered with the entire class. Tier 2 represents a small group of students, in this case those who have been identified as needing additional support. Tier 3 students receive intensive, individualized support.

	Current Instructional Model Practices		
Trauma-informed Practices Key Tenets	**Setting clear objectives**	**Giving students real-world application of learning**	**Interact meaningfully with every student**
Getting to know students on a personal level			Plan for 1:1 weekly check-ins with Tier 3 students during study hour
Weekly restorative circles	Help students understand goals of the weekly circles with Tier 2 students		
Social/emotional development	Work with counselor to set personal objectives with Tier 3 students for Positive Behavior Interventions and Supports (PBIS)	Highlight key social and emotional learning (SEL) chapters and have students journal when someone might use these lessons (Tier 1 or 2)	Highlight when students show growth in positive behavior (Tier 1)

Tool 13: Dialogue Exercise—Why are we doing what we're doing?

Once a particular model becomes an integrated part of your school culture, we encourage you to occasionally revisit the "why" behind the model to ensure that implementation stays fresh and to keep from getting lockstep in the model—or running through the motions without thinking about why you're doing what you're doing.

Every semester or so, revisit the following reflection questions, inserting new areas of focus as you see fit.

- What new research is emerging that might expand our current use of _____?
- Where in my lessons have I found it most effective to use the practice of _____? When has it not been as effective?
- What are our latest performance assessments indicating about our practices?
- How has my thinking about _____ changed in the past six months?
- What worked for me last year that seems to be not working as well this year? What ideas do I have for why this might be so?
- Where do I feel our practice or understanding of _____ varies the most from classroom to classroom?
- What "why" questions have I asked of my teaching lately?

Note: For more about sparking curiosity in teaching, we recommend *Unstuck: How Curiosity, Peer Coaching, and Teaming Can Change Your School* (Goodwin, Gibson, Lewis, & Rouleau, 2018).

Chapter 8: Doing the right things right

Barbara is trying to decide whether to stop pushing the instructional model or to continue in spite of the naysayers. She recalls running into Julia at a district leaders' meeting and hearing how she was implementing her model. Her process had been much slower and had involved many more thought leaders in her school, yet their progress and impact on student learning had made headlines both locally and at a recent educational conference.

"If I could just go back in time and hit the 'reset' button," she muttered to herself, "I would do this so differently. Complete an audit of available models, have a team of leaders choose the one that best fits our needs, get lots of buy-in…"

As she ponders, she begins to wonder if such a reset could be possible. Could she admit her mistakes to her community, then start from the beginning? Re-energized, she reaches out to Julia to fully understand her process and to see if she has any words of advice. At the beginning of the following school year, she will hold a series of meetings with her faculty and with parents where she will be candid about her missteps and take ownership of how ineffective her process was. She will invite a small group of teacher leaders, including some of her strongest adversaries and supporters, to be a part of this group, where they will begin taking a hard look at their greatest instructional concerns.

From that point forward, she will closely follow a process similar to Julia's and will have similar celebrations in the coming years. ~

At this point, you might be thinking this seems like a lot of work. You'd be right. It *is* a lot of work. Yet it's the *right* work. Along with curriculum, instruction is the heart of schooling—something you provide every day, in every classroom, to every student. It's also something you can control (perhaps even more than your curriculum, which may be mandated by your state, district, or other agencies). Moreover, great instruction can motivate learners and help them develop confidence in their abilities, and thus address other key leverage points in your school. So, in many ways, instruction represents your core business as a school.

A pizza parlor parable: A school improvement fable

To illustrate, imagine you have a friend who owns a pizza parlor. One day she calls and tells you that her restaurant—her lifelong dream into which she has poured all of her savings—is failing; if she doesn't do something soon, she'll have to lay off her entire staff and declare bankruptcy.

She feels like she's tried everything—adding new varieties of pizza to the menu, redecorating, and motivating staff by trying to a be a "cool boss" who gives them lots of flexibility and encourages them to express themselves at work. Desperate for help, she asks for your advice on what to do to keep her restaurant afloat.

Without knowing much about the restaurant business, you ask questions about her location (is she in a convenient spot? is there enough parking?), her advertising (do people know about her business?), her pricing (is she too expensive? too cheap to cover her expenses?), her customers (what do they like? do they come back repeatedly?), and her competitors (are there lots of other pizza parlors in town?). At some point, though, you realize there's only so much advice you can give from afar. So, hearing her desperation, you offer to pay the restaurant a visit as a "secret shopper" to see if you can figure out what's going on.

When you arrive at the restaurant, you immediately notice that while some of the staff look professional, others do not. The hostess, in particular, greets you with unwashed hair, flip flops, and a T-shirt emblazoned with an edgy (if not offensive) image. After only a minute or two, your waiter, a sharply dressed, charming young man with a nice smile and friendly personality, greets you. Before taking your order, he advises you against several varieties of pizza on the menu and points to a couple "tried-and-true" varieties that have long been customer favorites.

After he takes your order, you hear customers at a nearby table complaining loudly that they've been seated for 20 minutes and no one has taken their order or even brought them water. Finally, a different waiter than yours emerges from what seems to have been a smoke break out back and gruffly takes the table's order. After he walks away, leaving angry patrons in his wake, you glance around the restaurant and notice several tables cluttered with dirty plates and glasses—no one has bussed them. Your waiter returns a moment later, bringing you a basket of breadsticks—"on the house," he explains, because he purposely delayed your order so the restaurant's best chef, who comes on duty in a few minutes, will make it. You also notice that, unable to locate a busboy, he takes it upon himself to clean off a nearby table.

Across the restaurant, you see a frustrated family send their pizza back to the kitchen, complaining it's undercooked—the cheese is still cold. When your pizza arrives several minutes later—apparently after the shift change in the kitchen—it's delicious, some of the best pizza you've ever had; you can taste your friend's flair for cooking in it and figure the chef who's on duty now must share her passion and attention to detail. When the check arrives, your waiter explains that on top of the free breadsticks, he also "comped" your drink to thank you for your patience.

Once in your car, you call your friend. "I think I see the problem," you say.

"We need a gimmick, don't we?" she replies, before you can offer your thoughts. "You know, like animatronic singing bears, roller-skating wait staff, or actors having Wild West gunfights."

Obviously, that's *not* the answer. You've seen firsthand that simply delivering what's *already good* (its bright spots) about the restaurant (good pizza and friendly service) with *greater consistency* is what matters most—and likely to keep customers coming back and the restaurant in the black. Singing bears, roller skaters, or gunslingers aren't going to help—they'll only be a distraction.

The point of this fable, as you've probably guessed by now, is that many underperforming schools, including those in chaos, often do something similar, overlooking the basics of quality and consistency. Instead, some school and system leaders imagine the key to success is doing something "innovative" and thus opt to implement the equivalent of singing bears—whether it's one-to-one laptop initiatives, personalized learning, or cross-curricular STEM (or STEAM) programs—which can be fine things to do *after* a school has developed a shared understanding of good instruction and the capacity to implement it with consistency. Simply dropping newfangled ideas or innovations into chaos will do little to improve the chaos—and probably only make it worse.

What happens when we get the right things right

Moreover, we've seen, firsthand, that schools usually don't need to do anything fancy to dramatically improve student learning. Often, "plain vanilla" reforms will do the trick—starting with simply ensuring effective teaching in every classroom. Here are a few success stories from a wide array of schools and districts.

Clarksville-Montgomery County School System, Tennessee

Over the course of several years, CMCSS, a fast-growing district with 39 schools and 35,600 students on the Tennessee-Kentucky border that had once been a high-performing district, noticed it had somehow slid to the middle of the pack among Tennessee's 140-plus school districts—largely because, in the estimation of then-superintendent B.J. Worthington and his leadership team, they weren't delivering consistent, high-quality instruction in classrooms. In a dual effort that focused both on improving instructional leadership (following the principles of McREL's Balanced Leadership® program) at the school level and adopting Explicit Direct Instruction in classrooms, the district began to see gains in student learning—slowly at first, but soon picking up speed as the flywheel began to turn. As of this writing, for four consecutive years CMCSS has demonstrated the highest student growth rates in the state of Tennessee and climbed from middle of the pack to the top among the state's 10 largest districts.

Gilcrest Elementary School, Colorado

In 2012, Gilcrest Elementary, a small rural school with a high-poverty student body (63% receiving free or reduced lunches) in a farming community on the Colorado high plains, was in trouble; mired in "turnaround status," it had just five years to improve or the staff and leadership would be replaced, or the school shut down altogether. National data show that when most schools face such dire consequences, they often scramble frantically to implement a flurry of improvements, yet rarely improve. "When I came to this school there were a lot of good intentions and a lot of expertise, but a lack of consistency," Principal Tad MacDonald told us. Working with McREL, he decided to take a more calm, measured approach—focusing first on helping teachers to unpack the state's standards so they understood what they were trying to teach. Then he ensured every teacher was following a common model for instruction—in this case McREL's model based on decades of research. Doing that ensured teachers were using real-time checks for understanding and adjusting instruction in the moment rather than waiting before it was too late to support struggling learners. The results? By 2017, Gilcrest students were demonstrating strong annual growth in learning, allowing the school to leap four levels from "turnaround" to a school with a performance plan. "I am … very happy with the growth and results at Gilcrest Elementary School," noted district superintendent Don Rangel. "In fact, the results are incredible."

West St. Paul-Mendota Heights-Eagan Area Schools, Minnesota

When this small (5,000-student) district on the south side of the St. Paul-Minneapolis metropolitan area began working with McREL to focus on instructional leadership in 2013, they soon saw the power of common professional vocabulary for teachers and leaders. In addition to developing a common template for school improvement planning, they adopted a common model for instruction (based on McREL's research on effective instruction) and created a cadre of district-level experts who could provide teachers with professional learning and coaching on the instructional model in their classrooms. Districtwide, student achievement rose in science by 3.6%, reading by 4.5%, and math by 7.6%—with even more dramatic gains in schools where leaders focused on ensuring consistency in use of the model. "The better the plan, and the truer the leader stays to the plan, the better the outcome," then-superintendent Nancy Allen-Mastro told us. "Seriousness around planning and follow-through has been a game-changer."

Lincoln Public Schools, Nebraska

Located in the heart of the heartland, LPS is a surprisingly diverse school district; its students speak 120 different languages at home and 46% receive free or reduced-price lunch. Every year, 800 new students and 400 new teachers join the fast-growing district, which led Sarah Salem, director of continuous improvement and professional learning, to realize she needed to help the district find an "instructional backbone" that would help its 3,500 teachers deliver consistent, high-quality instruction. Over a period of three years, the district focused on implementing McREL's model of learning with a particular focus on developing teachers' knowledge and skills in setting objectives, providing feedback, reinforcing effort, providing recognition, and engaging students in productive cooperative learning groups. As the emphasis on better instruction began to permeate schools, professional learning community conversations focused increasingly on student learning and teaching practices with teachers becoming more intentional about their instruction (considering not only *what* they're doing, but also *why* they're doing it) and setting their own objectives for improvement. "It's truly remarkable when I go into classrooms and ask students what they are learning, and they immediately look at the objective and can put it in their own words," Salem told us. Just as remarkable are the districtwide gains in student learning—with the number of students demonstrating proficiency rising seven, five, and six percentage points in third, fourth, and fifth grades, respectively.

Sublette County School District #1, Wyoming

Shortly after adopting new evaluation instruments for principals and teachers, Jay Harnack, superintendent of a district that spans a geographic area roughly the combined size of Delaware and Rhode Island, realized he needed to adopt a twofold approach to improvement to stem the tide of declining achievement among the district's rapidly growing, diversifying, and increasingly mobile student population. He would need to help principals become better instructional leaders while ensuring greater consistency and quality among classroom teachers by adopting a common model for classroom instruction. To ensure tight alignment across the district, he ensured leaders attended teacher professional learning sessions, and several teachers from each school also attended leadership development sessions. This helped teachers to understand that district-level initiatives were aimed, first and foremost, at supporting them in the classroom. "You can draw a line from our strategic plan all the way down to classroom practices," he noted. By achieving this clarity, the district also achieved "stair-step" like gains every year in multiple indicators. For example, the average ACT score among its increasingly diverse high school students rose from 19.4 in 2010 to 21.9 in 2013 and the district, which had once been on the decline, received the highest accreditation ratings in the state of Wyoming—on par with the highest-rated districts nationwide. "There's so much white noise out there about everything other than what needs to be done, it's easy to lose track," Harnack told us. "But we have found what works for our district. Our test scores show, when implemented with fidelity, aligned, research-based [leadership and instructional] practices lead to improvement—not in my elementary school, not in my middle school, not in my high school, but in all three, almost in lockstep. You can't beat that."

The power of instructional leadership

You've probably noticed a common theme among these success stories: nearly all of these schools and districts focused on not only creating more consistent, high-quality classroom instruction, but also, ensuring more consistent, supportive *instructional leadership*. The two, of course, go hand-in-hand, which is why we've written this book for school leadership teams. In our experience, we've seen that applying an instructional model in classrooms requires strong, supportive leadership.

Earlier, we described the importance of using data not as a window—to peer out on what others are doing (right or wrong), but also as a mirror, reflecting back on our own practices. So, we'd remind you to do that continually as you consider how well teachers are applying your chosen instructional model in their classrooms. Certainly, take a moment to celebrate the bright spots and reflect on what you did as a leadership team—what conditions you created to allow those bright spots to happen. You'll want to build on those bright spots, of course. At the same time, when you see missed opportunities or opportunities for improvement, reflect on what you can do better next time as leaders. For example, did you not attend the professional learning sessions yourselves? What message might that have sent? Did you give teachers enough opportunities to practice and apply the new learning in their classrooms? Do enough to support peer coaching? Keep the effort front-and-center in faculty meetings?

A key takeaway here is that as multiple studies have shown, your actions as leaders are tremendously important. For example, a meta-analysis of 27 studies (Robinson, Lloyd, & Rowe, 2008) found that instructional leadership behaviors—including actively engaging in teacher learning, focusing on improving instruction, and guiding curriculum planning and enactment—had a powerful effect on student achievement (ES = 0.42)—nearly four times the effect size of what are sometimes called *transformational leadership* behaviors (e.g., building school culture and fostering shared purpose) (ES = 0.11). This led the researchers to conclude that "the closer leaders are to the core business of teaching and learning, the more likely they are to make a difference to students" (p. 636).

So, in picking up this book, you've chosen to focus on the right work. In fact, for many schools, there is no more important work than ensuring consistency and quality in the delivery of learning experiences for students. What's more, research (and our experience) shows that unlike the myriad things you *cannot* control about your school or students' lives, you *can* have a powerful influence on what happens in classrooms by focusing simply and squarely on improving instruction through the use of an instructional model.

A "hack" for better learning—and schools

We'd also like to note something we've noticed about schools where leaders and teachers work together to apply instructional models to achieve greater quality and consistency in learning experiences for students. Far from being places of drudgery with leaders beating the drum to keep everyone in line, they are *joyful* places. Yes, it will take work. Yes, there will be frustrating moments. Yes, you may need to have some challenging conversations. But in the end, it will be worth it.

Remember why you started down this path in the first place. It was never to frustrate teachers, suck the joy out of learning, or add one more thing to everyone's plate. Rather, it was to focus on one thing that you can do together to create a school where students are engaged in learning and where adults feel a sense of accomplishment in changing students' lives, where you see bright spots in every classroom, and where students experience joy in learning. In other words, the model itself isn't the end goal here, but rather the *means* to an end—likely something deeper and more important, reflecting the shared moral purpose you identified back in chapter 4.

Ultimately, the purpose of an instructional model is to demystify teaching and decomplexify school improvement. Learning your model may take a few weeks or months; mastering it may take a lifetime. Ultimately, like an athlete improving her tennis stroke by comparing herself to a pro, an aspiring artist learning to paint with precision by recreating the work of a Dutch master, or a garage band honing its skills by covering others' songs, you're apt to find it much easier than *not* having a model, which would force you to cast about to figure out what works. As in so many other areas of our lives that we'd like to improve, from our mood to our finances to our weight, the fix may not always be easy, but it is, in essence, simple.

Indeed, in many ways, using an effective instructional model to design and deliver better learning experiences for students serves as a handy "hack" for improving classroom instruction and school performance—something to shorten your learning curve as school leaders and professional educators, getting you from where you are to where you want to be a little more directly and efficiently. It's not the end of your journey, of course. Recall that Madeline Hunter saw her own instructional model as a "launching pad" to more creative and effective teaching. We agree. And we hope that you'll use this book as a launching pad to create classrooms and schools where students can experience curiosity, challenge themselves, and flourish as learners.

Appendix: If you're on your own

Throughout this book, we have suggested steps and processes with the assumption that the initiative to implement an instructional model starts at the leadership level or at least has leadership support. There are times, however, when adoption of an improved instructional framework starts at the grassroots level. While this is often a longer and more difficult process (change is always easier when others change with us), here's some guidance on how to prove the model's effectiveness, get peers on board, and make the case to your leadership team.

Whether you recently learned of an effective model from a colleague or you came from another district that was successfully using one, you may be seeking to apply an instructional model in your own classroom (and/or hoping to encourage others to use it in their classrooms as well), yet aren't in a position of authority. If this is the case, we recommend four key steps that will give you the greatest chance of success in helping others to consider a new model:

1. Take the time to establish yourself as an effective instructor.
2. Keep meticulous instructional notes and corresponding growth data so that you can show the model's effectiveness.
3. Find nonthreatening ways to share what is working in your classroom.
4. Learn key tactics on leading or influencing without positional authority.

Take the time to establish yourself as an effective instructor

How many of us have seen someone new join a community and instantly begin complaining about how things are "done around here"? We have watched helplessly as colleagues brashly put down current procedures, talked incessantly about how much better their previous workplace used to do things, and inadvertently made themselves persona non grata within the first few months of joining a team. (And if we have ever been that person, please accept our humblest apologies!)

Even with the best of intentions, a common mistake people make is not taking the time to cultivate their reputation for excellence before suggesting changes. No matter your success or your role in your past workplace, building trust and credibility among new colleagues takes time. Give yourself and your colleagues some time to go through this process before you begin suggesting new models or procedures. It may take a year or two before your work begins to speak for itself. You don't want to kill your initiative before it ever has a chance.

One of the best indicators that you have set the stage for change is when colleagues start asking for the secrets to your success. Do fellow teachers ask if you will share your lesson plans? Do they ask if they can observe in your classroom? Have they started asking for feedback on their lessons? If so, you may be ready to take your model to your leadership team to ask if they would be open to learning more about what you have implemented.

Keep meticulous notes and track growth data to show the model's effectiveness

As you are establishing your effectiveness as an instructor, keep meticulous instructional notes and growth data as you work with your students. It's far more effective to show growth over time than to simply have students who perform at high levels. Consider journaling so that, beyond just quantitative test scores, you also have qualitative data that show what you observed, tactics you tried, and how students responded.

If you're considering, or experimenting with, different models, meticulous note-taking will also help you to compare the impact of each model and help you to avoid any unconscious bias when implementing the models. It's easy, even with the best of intentions, to give our "favorite" models a better chance of succeeding than those with which we are less enamored; collecting our thoughts in a systematic way can help us to remain more objective and avoid skewing our use of any particular model to confirm our biases. Specifically, you may wish to include observations in your journal about the strengths of each model, elements that are challenging to implement, your students' responses to it, and the perceived benefits of the model—why you think some teachers might prefer one model over another.

Find nonthreatening ways to share what is working in your classroom

If you feel (and others would agree) that you have established yourself as a trusted colleague, you may wish to find non-threatening ways to begin sharing your model, strategies, and data—likely starting with casual sharing during faculty or team meetings. Making the leap from a quiet leader to one who actively promotes what she believes takes finesse, of course. Here, you might find it helpful to consider the principles of the diffusion of innovations identified years ago by Everett Rogers (2003), who tracked how farmers shared and adopted new farming techniques. Specifically, he noticed people were more apt to adopt an innovation when a handful of conditions were present:

- **Compatibility**—when people see how a new idea is consistent with their core values (e.g., "You know how it's important to us that students are engaged in deep learning? Well, I've been trying some things in my classroom that really seem to be doing that.")
- **Advantage**—when people see how the new approach will make things better (e.g., "I've noticed that I've really been able to keep kids focused and on-track—way more than they used to be.")
- **Observability**—when people can see the idea or approach in action (e.g., "I'd be happy to share with you what I'm doing—or even have you come in and watch one of my lessons.")

- **Simplicity**—when the new concept or approach is easy to understand (e.g., "It's actually a really simple, six-stage process for lesson design; it didn't take me long to learn at all.")
- **Trial-ability**—when people can experiment with the new idea or approach before adopting it fully (e.g., "You could try it for a single lesson—I'd be happy to give you one of my lesson plans.")

Learn how to lead and influence without positional authority

Not having positional authority needn't be a problem. Many articles and books have been written about how to influence "up" or to bring about change when you don't have positional authority. Cohen and Bradford's *Influence Without Authority* (1990) is a classic. It cites the importance of identifying the goals and motivations of your leaders (i.e., what keeps them up at night), and aligning your mission with meeting those goals. Once you're clear about the goals of your leadership team—and have some confidence that what you're doing aligns with those goals—you might invite one or more members of the leadership team to visit your classroom. Initially, the contact will just be about providing you with feedback (e.g., "I really love the emphasis you've been putting on critical thinking in our staff meetings and professional learning sessions; I'd love to show you what I've been doing in my classroom and get your feedback on how to improve"). Likely, they'll see what you're doing and want to know more. But don't be discouraged if they don't do cartwheels or sing your praises to everyone they know—the timing may simply be wrong. Keep at it and continue to frame what you're doing in terms of your school's and leadership team's goals.

Along similar lines, it's also a good idea to build so-called relationship capital among your colleagues by showing others in your building that you're willing to help, curious about what they're doing, and committed to *their* success. Sometimes, especially if you're new to a building, you'll want to spend months doing that before ever asking anything of your colleagues. In fact, you may find there's never a right time to offer unsolicited advice; rather, by simply being helpful and showing passion for what you're doing, others will eventually express interest in your lessons and your approach to teaching and learning.

Your purpose with all of these tactics is not to be manipulative or cunning, but simply to be a good colleague and teammate, sharing ideas and helping others to succeed. With this in mind, we'd encourage you to "do you"—that is, play to your own professional strengths and personality. In his book *The Tipping Point*, Gladwell (2000) identifies three different types of influencers—*connectors* (those who are naturally outgoing and easily connect with many different people), *mavens* (those who command respect by being experts on particular topics and demonstrating willingness to help others), and *salespeople* (those whose natural charm and charisma make others simply want to agree with them). You might want to consider which of these roles comes most naturally to you and play to those strengths as you seek to encourage schoolwide use of an instructional model—and also identify others in your school who reflect these roles and connect with them, so that together, you can generate interest and buy-in for using an instructional model in your school.

Final reflection and checklist

Reflecting on your progress

1. Why do I feel so strongly about this particular model? Can I describe in a short phrase or sentence the difference it's made in my classroom?

2. How might I employ the principles of the diffusion of innovation (Compatibility, Advantage, Observability, Simplicity, Trial-ability) to encourage others to adopt the model?

3. What current influences do I have with my fellow teachers? With school leaders?

4. With whom do I have strong personal ties? Weak ones? In what ways could I be helpful to my colleagues?

5. What motivates my principal and/or school leadership team? How might I show her/him/them how using an instructional model could help us to achieve our shared goals?

6. Would I consider myself a *maven*, *connector*, or *salesperson*? Who in my school fits those roles? How might I connect with them to create a "movement" in the school?

Checklist for staying the course and influencing up

☐ Create your system of tracking student progress and capturing your instructional notes.

☐ Read books, articles, or watch instructional videos on "influencing up."

☐ Create a small group of colleagues who share your interest in an instructional model.

References

Barber, M., & Mourshed, M. (2007, September). *How the world's best performing school systems come out on top*. London: McKinsey & Company.

Bendall, R. C. A., Galpin, A., Marrow, L. P., & Cassidy, S. (2016). Cognitive style: Time to experiment. *Frontiers in Psychology, 7*. Retrieved from https://www.frontiersin.org/articles/10.3389/fpsyg.2016.01786/full

Bill & Melinda Gates Foundation. (2015). *Teachers know best: Making data work for teachers and students*. Seattle, WA: Author.

Bloom, B. S. (Ed.). (1956). *Taxonomy of educational objectives: The classification of educational goals. Handbook 1: Cognitive domain*. New York: Longman.

Bridges, W. (1991). *Managing transitions: Making the most of change*. Reading, MA: Addison-Wesley.

Bryk, A. S., Gomez, L., Grunow, A., & LeMahieu, P. (2015). *Learning to improve: How America's schools can get better at getting better*. Cambridge, MA: Harvard Education Publishing.

Bryk, A. S., Sebring, P. B., Kerbow, D., Rollow, S., & Easton, J. Q. (1998). *Charting Chicago School Reform: Democratic Localism as a Lever for Change*. Boulder, CO: Westview Press.

Chenoweth, K. (2007). *It's being done: Academic success in unexpected schools*. Cambridge, MA: Harvard Education Press.

Chenoweth, K. (2009). *How it's being done: Urgent lessons from unexpected schools*. Cambridge, MA: Harvard Education Press.

Cohen, A. R., & Bradford, D. L. (1990). *Influence without authority*. New York, NY: J. Wiley.

Coffield, F., Moseley, D., Hall, E., & Ecclestone, K. (2004). *Learning styles and pedagogy in post-16 learning: A systematic and critical review*. London, England: Learning & Skills Research Centre.

Covey, S. (1989). *The 7 habits of highly effective people*. New York: Free Press.

Cuban, L. (1984). *How teachers taught: Constancy and change in American classrooms*. New York, NY: Longman.

Darling-Hammond, L., Amrein-Beardsley, A., Haertel, E., & Rothstein, J. (2012). Evaluating teacher evaluation. *Phi Delta Kappan, 93*(6), 8–15.

Datnow, A., Park, V., & Kennedy-Lewis, B. (2013). Affordances and constraints in the context of teacher collaboration for the purpose of data use. *Journal of Educational Administration, 51*(3), 341–362.

Dean, C. B., Hubbell, E. R., Pitler, H., & Stone, B. (2012). *Classroom instruction that works* (2nd ed.). Alexandria, VA: ASCD.

Dobrowolski, P. (2012, January 10). *Draw your future* [Lecture]. Retrieved from https://www.youtube.com/watch?v=zESeeaFDVSw&vl=en

Ericsson, K. A., Prietula, M. J., & Cokely, E. T. (2007). The making of an expert. *Harvard Business Review, 85*(7/8), 114–121.

Finnigan, K., Daly, A. J., & Che, J. (2012). Mind the gap: Learning, trust, and relationships in an underperforming urban system. *American Journal of Education, 119*(1), 41–71.

Fullan, M. (2001). *Leading in a culture of change.* San Francisco, CA: Jossey-Bass.

Gladwell, M. (2000). *The tipping point: How little things can make a big difference.* New York, NY: Little Brown.

Goodwin, B. (2011). *Simply better: Doing what matters most to change the odds for student success.* Alexandria, VA: ASCD.

Goodwin, B. (2018). *Student learning that works: How brain science informs a student learning model.* Denver, CO: McREL International.

Goodwin, B., Cameron, G., & Hein, H. (2015). *Balanced leadership for powerful learning: Tools for achieving success in your school.* Alexandria, VA: ASCD.

Goodwin, B., Gibson, T., Lewis, D., & Rouleau, K. (2018). *Unstuck: How curiosity, peer coaching, and teaming can change your school.* Alexandria, VA: ASCD.

Goodwin, B., & Hubbell, E. R. (2013). *The 12 touchstones of good teaching: A checklist for staying focused every day.* Alexandria, VA: ASCD.

Goodwin, B., Rouleau, K., & Lewis, D. (2018). *Curiosity works: A guidebook for moving your school from improvement to innovation.* Denver, CO: McREL International.

Guskey, T. R. (2007). Where do you want to get to? *The Learning Professional, 38*(2), 32–37, 78.

Hall, G., & Hord, S. (2015). *Implementing change: Patterns, principles, and potholes* (4th ed.) Austin, TX: Southwest Educational Development Laboratory (SEDL).

Hattie, J. (2011). *Visible learning for teachers: Maximizing impact on learning.* London, England: Routledge.

Heath, C., & Heath, D. (2010). *Switch: How to change things when change is hard.* New York, NY: Crown Business.

Herrmann, N. (1998). *Twenty years of thinking about the thinking brain. A special summary of learning outcomes.* Unpublished document.

Hines, T. (1987). Left brain/right brain mythology and implications for management and training. *The Academy of Management Review, 12*(4), 600–606. Retrieved from http://www.jstor.org/stable/258066

Hofman, P., Goodwin, B., & Kahl, S. (2015). *Re-balancing assessment: Placing formative and performance assessment at the heart of learning and accountability.* Denver, CO: McREL International.

Hord, S. M., Stiegelbauer, S. M., Hall, G. E., & George, A. A. (2006). *Measuring implementation in schools: Innovation configurations.* Austin, TX: Southwest Educational Development Laboratory (SEDL).

Horn, I. S., Kane, B. D., & Wilson, J. (2015). Making sense of student performance data: Data use logics and mathematics teachers' learning opportunities. *American Educational Research Journal, 52*(2), 208–242.

Hunter, M. (1985). What's wrong with Madeline Hunter? *Educational Leadership, 42*(5), 57–60.

Jackson, K., & Makarin, A. (2018). Can online off-the-shelf lessons improve student outcomes? Evidence from a field experiment. *American Economic Journal, 10*(3), 226–254.

Joyce, B., & Showers, B. (2002). *Student achievement through staff development* (3rd ed.). Alexandria, VA: ASCD.

Kahneman, D. (2011). *Thinking, fast and slow.* New York, NY: Farrar, Straus & Giroux.

Kulik, C. L. C., Kulik, J. A., Bangert-Drowns, R. L., & Slavin, R. E. (1990). Effectiveness of mastery learning programs: A meta-analysis. *Review of Educational Research, 60*(2), 265–299.

Larson, E. (2017, March 23). 3 best practices for high performance decision-making teams. *Forbes.* Retrieved from https://www.forbes.com/sites/eriklarson/2017/03/23/3-best-practices-for-high-performance-decision-making-teams/#5596031cf971

Marzano, R., Waters, T., & McNulty, B. (2005). *School leadership that works: From research to results.* Alexandria, VA: ASCD.

Mathews, J. (2011, December 18). New teacher decries lesson plan gap. *The Washington Post.* Retrieved from https://www.washingtonpost.com/blogs/class-struggle/post/new-teacher-decries-lesson-plan-gap/2011/12/17/gIQAt0C50O_blog.html

McREL (2005). *Schools that "beat the odds"* (Technical brief). Denver, CO: Author.

National Council on Teacher Quality. (2014). *Standard 11: Lesson planning: What Consumers need to know about teacher preparation.* Washington, DC: Author.

Pianta, R. C., Belsky, J., Houts, R., & Morrison, F. (2007). Opportunities to learn in America's elementary classrooms. *Science, 315*(5820), 1795–1796.

Pomerance, L., Greenberg, J., & Walsh, K. (2016). *Learning about learning: What every new teacher needs to know.* Washington, DC: National Council on Teacher Quality.

Public Impact. (2007). *School turnarounds: A review of the cross-sector evidence on dramatic organizational improvement.* Lincoln, IL: Author.

Reynolds, D., Stringfield, S., & Schaffer, E. (2001). *The high reliability schools project: Some preliminary results and analysis.* Retrieved from https://www.researchgate.net/publication/266488793_The_High_Reliability_Schools_Project_Some_Preliminary_Results_and_Analyses

Robinson, V. M. J., Lloyd, C. A., & Rowe, K. J. (2008). The impact of leadership on student outcomes: An analysis of the differential effects of leadership types. *Educational Administration Quarterly, (44)*5, 635–674.

Rogers, E. M. (2003). *Diffusions of innovations* (5th ed). New York, NY: Simon & Schuster.

Rowe, M. B. (1986). Wait time: Slowing down may be a way of speeding up! *Journal of Teacher Education, 37*(1), 43–50.

Sanders, W. L., & Rivers, J. C. (1996). *Cumulative and residual effects of teachers on future student academic achievement.* Knoxville, TN: University of Tennessee Value-Added Research and Assessment Center.

Schmoker, M. (2014, September 23). The Common Core is not ready. *Education Week.* Retrieved from http://www.edweek.org/ew/articles/2014/09/24/05schmoker.h34.html

Sinek, S. (2009). How great leaders inspire action [Video file]. Retrieved from https://www.ted.com/talks/simon_sinek_how_great_leaders_inspire_action#t-4539

Sinek, S. (2011). *Start with why.* New York, NY: Portfolio.

U.S. Department of Education, Office of Planning, Evaluation and Policy Development. (2011). *Teachers' ability to use data to inform instruction: Challenges and supports.* Washington, DC: Author.

Willingham, D. T., Hughes, E. M., & Dobolyi, D. G. (2015). The scientific status of learning styles theories. *Teaching of Psychology, 42*(3), 266–271. Retrieved from https://career.ucsf.edu/sites/career.ucsf.edu/files/Article%20UCSF%20SEJC%20January%202017.pdf

Young, V. (2006). Teachers' use of data: Loose coupling, agenda setting, and team norms. *American Journal of Education, 112*(4), 521–548.

About the Authors

Elizabeth Ross Hubbell is an educator, author, and speaker with more than 20 years' experience across many levels of education. She currently serves as senior program manager at Academic Impressions, where she designs professional learning experiences for higher education. Her primary topics of interest include women's leadership and new innovations in student success and retention. Prior to joining Academic Impressions, Elizabeth served as a K–12 consultant with McREL International, focusing on instructional strategies and technologies. She is a co-author, with Bryan Goodwin, of *The 12 Touchstones of Good Teaching: A Checklist for Staying Focused Every Day* and co-author of *Classroom Instruction That Works* (2nd ed.). She has presented at the ACEL, ASCD, ISTE, Colorado TIE, Learning Forward, SREB, NSBA's T+L, and EARCOS conferences. Elizabeth is a former Montessori teacher.

Bryan Goodwin is president and CEO of McREL International. For 21 years at McREL, he has translated research into practice, scanning the world for new insights and best practices on teaching and leading, and has helped educators everywhere adapt them to address their own challenges. A frequent conference presenter, he is the author of *Out of Curiosity: Restoring the Power of Hungry Minds for Better Schools, Workplaces, and Lives* and *Simply Better: Doing What Matters Most to Change the Odds for Student Success*, as well as co-author of *Curiosity Works: A Guidebook for Moving Your School from Improvement to Innovation*, *Unstuck: How Curiosity, Peer Coaching, and Teaming Can Change Your School*, *Balanced Leadership for Powerful Learning: Tools for Achieving Success in Your School*, and *The 12 Touchstones of Good Teaching: A Checklist for Staying Focused Every Day*. Before joining McREL in 1998, Bryan was a college instructor, a high school teacher, and a business journalist.